BOLD TRACKS
Skiing for the Disabled

Hal O'Leary, P.S.I.A., N.H.S.R.A.
Director, Winter Park Handicap Program

Editor ▌ **Mary M. Meinig**
Art Director ▌ **Ann W. Douden**

CORDILLERA PRESS, INC.
Publishers in the Rockies

Warning: Skiing is a dangerous activity and should be done only with qualified instruction, proper equipment, and one's own common sense. Instructors, students, and others using this manual are reminded that they participate in skiing solely at their own risk.

Library of Congress Cataloging-in-Publication Data

O'Leary, Hal.
   Bold tracks.

   Bibliography: p.
   Includes index.
   1. Skiing for the handicapped — Study and teaching — United States.
I. Meinig, Mary M.   II. Title.
GV854.33.O54   1987   796.93'02408   87-33132
ISBN 0-917895-22-3

Printed in U.S.A.

Production   Meinig & Douden, writing and design
      Evergreen, Colorado (303) 674-0597

Marj Leggitt, illustrator
Gus Allen Alavezos, flipbook illustrator / Agent: Carol Guenzi
Gary Hall, Focus II Studio, photography
Jeanne Smith, Steve Stone, location photography
Richard M. Kohen, Shadow Canyon Graphics, mechanicals
Campro Systems, typography

Cover illustration of Winter Park Resort by Ann W. Douden

Special graphic effects were used to create the photograph on the title page. A combination of a mezzotint and a photographic outline give the photograph its unique look. Special effects are by Campro Systems, Denver, Colorado.

Cordillera Press, Inc.
Post Office Box 3699
Evergreen, Colorado 80439
(303) 670-3010

Published in cooperation with the Winter Park Sports & Learning Center, Inc. and generously funded in part by the Frost Foundation.

TABLE OF CONTENTS

4   ACKNOWLEDGMENTS
5   PREFACE
6   INTRODUCTION
7   DEDICATION
8   THE PHILOSOPHY
9   ABOUT HAL O'LEARY
10 ABOUT THE WINTER PARK HANDICAP PROGRAM
14 HISTORY OF HANDICAP SKIING
    TEACHING METHODS
18 American Teaching System
30 Three Track
42 Amputations
44 Four Track
56 Cerebral Palsy
62 Visually Impaired
72 Hearing Impaired
78 Developmentally Disabled
82 Sit Ski
88 Mono-Ski
96 Disabled Senior Citizens
98 ADAPTIVE EQUIPMENT
    PROGRAM DEVELOPMENT
104 Fund Raising
108 Volunteers
111 Sample Forms
119 Handicapped Competition Program
120 SKIING TERMINOLOGY
    DISABILITIES: DEFINITIONS
122 Arthritis
123 Cancer: Leukemia, Sarcoma
    Cerebral Palsy
124 Developmentally Disabled
      Mentally Retarded
125   Down's Syndrome
      Autism
126   Epilepsy
127 Diabetes
    Friedreich's Ataxia
128 Head Injury
131 Learning Disabled
132 Multiple Sclerosis
    Muscular Dystrophy
133 Spina Bifida
134 Spinal Cord Injuries
141 MEDICAL GLOSSARY
142 MEDICATIONS
144 RESOURCES
149 HAL'S PALS
151 INDEX

4 | ACKNOWLEDGEMENTS

Susan Anderson, HAL'S PALS

Dr. Tom Balazy, Craig Hospital, Denver; consultant on spinal cord

John Borelli, consultant on visually impaired

Katie Branch, overview on volunteers

Anne Bulkley, photography

Pat Campanello, instructor

Cindy Castellano, fund raising and grants

Amy Cavanaugh, instructor

Paul DiBello, Director of Handicapped Competition

Gigi Dominguez, Program Coordinator, Handicap Program

Beth Fox, instructor

Nancy Haisley, Executive Secretary, Handicap Program

Jane Hansbery, instructor

Susan Hildebrecht, instructor

Homer Jennings, national coach

Pat and Gene Kayser, instructors

Cale Kenney, updated history

Hal Leith, consultant on hearing impaired

Betty Lessard, history

Carol Page, R.P.T., consultant on cerebral palsy and spina bifida

Emily Quinn, sit ski

Mike Rantz, instructor

M'el Reum, program history

Jim Richardson, instructor

Joan Spalding, program history

Jan Stokosa, prosthetics

Carol Wiechman, Rich St. Denis, Rick Ruscio, Gini Bradley, Kirk Parkhurst, Linda Becker; The Breckenridge Outdoor Education Center; mono-ski

Karen Witt, instructor

Woody Witte, Kenny Lacombe, mono-ski equipment

John Woodruff, film maker

The Pioneers (1968-1970)

Florence Britton, volunteer

Col. Paul W. Brown, Chief of Orthopedics, Fitzsimmons General Hospital, Denver, Colorado

Nan Gray, volunteer

Ed Lucks, head ski instructor, Arapahoe Basin

Virginia McMurtry, Regional Coordinator, fundraiser, volunteer

Dr. Duane Messner, Chief Adviser, Children's Hospital rehabilitation program at Winter Park

M'el Reum, volunteer

Willy Schaeffler, Director of Ski School, Arapahoe Basin

Dr. William F. Stanek, Director, Amputee Center, Children's Hosptial, Denver, Colorado

"Willie" Williams, R.N., Outpatient Coordinator of Rehabilitation and Orthopedics, Children's Hospital

5 | PREFACE

Someone once said, ''If God had meant us to ski, he would have given us feet with metal edges.''

As every instructor knows, learning to ski is essentially mastering the use of special equipment and highly developed skills to overcome various natural difficulties.

The skier uses attachments called skis to compensate for the inadequate length of his feet.

He uses special boots as a supporting prosthesis to overcome the inadequate rigidity of his ankles.

A skier must develop skills to keep him upright against the pull of gravity.

When you consider the problems we have to overcome, we're all handicapped skiers.

Cale Kenney, member of U.S. Disabled Ski Team.

6 | INTRODUCTION

This manual is designed to be used by the people and places involved in teaching the handicapped to ski; program developers, ski resort owners, fund raisers, program directors and managers, clinicians, instructors and volunteers.

The teaching core of the book covers the different techniques of skiing for the disabled: three track, four track, cerebral palsy (or two track), sit skiing and skiing for the visually and hearing impaired. Other disabilities are covered by association and adaptation.

We use the American Teaching System as the basis of our instruction and adapt it to each individual. We have included information from the current ATS publication as our first teaching section. A fuller reference is in the Resources list. Adaptive teaching techniques along with adaptive equipment form the cornerstones of our operation.

We repeat some of our major points about teaching in each of the sections for the benefit of the reader who is concentrating on a specific area or disability.

For everyone's benefit and understanding, we have added a major "medical section," where you will find definitions and explanations of the various disabilities. We have also compiled some glossaries of common and specialized terms, including skiing terminology and the language of adaptive equipment.

Finally, we tried to anticipate and answer your questions with some specifics about our Program, fund raising, the role of volunteers and our philosophy.

"We studied your program at great length — on the slopes and in the office — and liked what we saw: a unique and enviable program."

Winter 1968-69, the first year of the handicap program at Arapahoe Basin. From the collection of Mrs. Virginia McMurtry.

DEDICATION

At Winter Park, there is an expert run straight down the face of the mountain called ''Retta's Run.'' It was named for Retta Stanley, a registered nurse at Children's Hospital in Denver and a very special person in the development of the Winter Park Handicap Program.

In the early stages of our fledgling program, Retta worked with disabled kids from Children's Hospital — many of them cancer victims — at Winter Park to conquer their disabilities with the freedom of the mountain and downhill skiing. She gave generously of herself as an invaluable volunteer in the program. She was my teacher as well, contributing greatly to my education about the disabled. Retta taught me to have compassion instead of pity, and she emphasized dignity at all times.

Then cancer struck Retta, and she lost her leg above the knee. Having no pity for any handicap, including her own, she became one of the first women three track national champions.

After battling cancer for eight years, Retta lost her life. Her strength, intelligence and compassion made a lasting impression on everyone she touched.

In Retta's memory, I dedicate this teaching manual, with great pride in what she brought to us all.

Hal O'Leary

Retta Stanley

Throughout this manual, watch Retta ski by flipping the outer right hand pages from front to back.

8 | THE PHILOSOPHY

Recreation. It is good for everyone. But for the handicapped, it is a significant factor in eliminating the web of obstacles that restrict a person with a disability. To the handicapped, skiing can mean adventure, exercise, growth, development, self-respect and independence.

Lack of mobility has always been the chief obstacle for the handicapped person. Most rehabilitation programs focus solely on regaining physical strength and range of motion, whereas handicap sports programs use athletic participation to rehabilitate a person both physically and emotionally. This is especially true in downhill skiing. The handicapped skier's self-esteem skyrockets when he realizes that he can not only participate but can do so on an equal basis with able-bodied counterparts.

Recreation does more than build self-confidence. It also helps to erase social barriers and retire myths held by society and replaces them with understanding of and sensitivity to a handicapped person's abilities. The increased mental fitness and physical coordination gained through skiing make the handicapped individual better able to be employed or to attend school on a full-time basis. Skiing can be a family-and-friends affair, bringing support and companionship to the handicapped skier.

It is an enormous delight to handicapped people to move with speed, grace and ease though their skiing. They often say things like: "If I can do this, I can do anything" or "I love the wind in my face and the feeling of motion. The mountain does it for me." But in fact, this person has accomplished something that he perhaps never dreamed he could do. He is skiing.

Fred Tassone, Viet Nam Veteran and former coach for the U.S. Disabled Ski Team.

"I was able to challenge myself and experience a very important personal success which carried over into all aspects of my life."

"And then there is the fun, growth, smiles, self-worth, confidence and risk-taking that our students experience ... and so much more."

9 | ABOUT HAL O'LEARY

Hal O'Leary came to Colorado from Canada armed with the unlikely combination of a business degree and a desire to work outdoors. He was a salaried ski instructor at Winter Park and volunteered to help with the amputee program when it first began.

Hal had to fight for funding and support for his handicap ski program as it grew and took shape. But he was tenacious, unwilling to give up. By 1970 he was Director of the program. His first manual, printed in 1973 under the title, ''The Winter Park Amputee Ski Teaching System,'' enjoyed numerous printings and was translated into Japanese, Swedish and Spanish. By 1974, Hal was running an independent, well established handicap ski program, and his accomplishments — and reputation — were growing. In 1981, Hal garnered the prestigious Gold Quill Award from the national ski press, for individuals who make significant contribution to the field of skiing. In 1982, a second major award — from the National Forest Service — came to Hal for his important utilization of forest land in the interests of the handicapped.

Hal seems to have a natural talent for relating to each skier on an individual basis, modifying techniques, equipment and instructional approach to the situation at hand. To his students, he has been teacher, counselor and confidant.

Today he is a self-taught but highly trained technician. He understands and articulates the disabilities he handles with the precision of a medical specialist. He excels in his understanding and use of adaptive equipment. He knows how to apply the skill of skiing to the art of human management. He is a consummate master at helping people to believe in their own abilities — and ultimately in themselves.

Hal O'Leary   PHOTO: DEBRA LEWIS

Hal travels across the United States, Canada and to countries abroad teaching and consulting with others about handicap programs. He has made numerous training films on teaching the disabled to ski. He has been a spokesman for his cause to government. In 1982, Hal wrote a ski teaching manual for the developmentally disabled, published by the national Special Olympics.

Yet Hal O'Leary claims: ''I have gotten so much more out of the Program than I have put into it.'' He may think so, but many a handicapped skier would say it's a draw.

Editor's Note | *The original handicap sports program began in 1968 at Arapahoe Basin, about 50 miles west of Denver. 15 children from the Amputee Clinic at Children's Hospital in Denver were paired with a group of Viet Nam veterans from Fitzsimmons General Hospital. A "buddy system" developed that utilized the psychology of mutual support and encouragement while instructors experimented with ski techniques and equipment. Fund raising and other program needs were handled by very committed volunteers who sought donations of all kinds locally and afar. In January of 1970, the program moved to Winter Park, where our story begins. The pioneering supporters are listed in the Acknowledgments.*

The Winter Park
HANDICAP
PROGRAM

It began in the 1969-70 season, with 23 children from Children's Hospital in Denver, Colorado. It is now the largest and most renowned skiing program for handicapped persons in the world. It accommodates students who have one, or several, of 45 different disabilities. How did it happen? Hal O'Leary likes to tell this story.

When Jerry Groswold, then Chairman of the Board of Trustees, received a telephone call in January, 1970 from Children's Hospital asking if Winter Park could pick up another ski area's cancelled handicap ski program, he responded to the need.

The next day, ski school owner George Engel approached the group of ski instructors of Winter Park, explained the situation and asked for volunteers. "Mine was the only hand that went up," Hal explains. Hal O'Leary was then a six-year veteran ski instructor from Canada.

The next day George gave him a piece of paper. "Here," he said, "you're in charge."

Hal quickly went to work. The youngsters were due in six days. He called the name on the paper — Willie Williams, a nurse at Children's Hospital — and obtained a pair of outriggers (short skis mounted to a crutch with a movable head). He took three days off from his regular job of teaching and taught himself to ski on three tracks, improvising techniques based on the American Teaching System.

The following Thursday was not your typical Colorado sun-filled day. It was gray and bleak. The wind was howling. When Hal skied into the midst of the 23 very cold amputees who were lying on the snow, some crying, he was bewildered. What to do now? From behind came a sharp voice commanding: "On your feet!" The children responded immediately. Later, Hal teased the nurse in his easy-going manner: "Willie, you could have said, 'Up on your foot,' since they only have one."

The dedication and camaraderie that developed between Hal, the volunteers and the children who came from the hospital were to last a long time, and from that time on, Hal was committed. "I saw joy on their faces when they moved on skis in a way they couldn't walk. Their motions were fluid and smooth, like regular skiers. I began to think of the value of skiing for other handicapped persons."

Saturday, March 6, 1971. Historical photo from the collection of Mrs. Virginia McMurtry.

"Willie" Williams, R.N., Outpatient Coordinator of Rehabilitation and Orthopedics, Children's Hospital, Denver, 1968-1981 (left) and Carol Page, R.P.T., Coordinator Handicapped Sports Program, Children's Hospital, Denver (right)

What began as fun and games for a few handicapped youngsters soon grew into a serious educational enterprise. With racing successes and media coverage, the Program's reputation spread and demand for its services increased. Soon a volunteer corps developed around the Program, and more emphasis was placed on the design and use of adaptive equipment. Funding and independence came in time.

The Winter Park Handicap Program has tremendous out-reaching qualities for its students. The social and recreational benefits help build new attitudes, new confidences and new lives.

The Program has created a positive effect not only on its students but also for the ski area and town of Winter Park. Many former students are now employees of the area or in the town. In Winter Park and in the Program, these people are not different. They are very much in the mainstream of this mountain community. Conversely, many normal employees of Winter Park choose to volunteer in the handicap program on their days off.

Through media coverage and international publicity, the Program has become known around the world and spread across the United States to Canada, South America, Europe and Australia and New Zealand,

The Program has demanded of itself the very best in handicap recreational instruction, in a caring, accepting atmosphere. The students respond in turn by demanding the best of themselves. Through shared effort there is the self-confidence and pride that come from knowing you have successfully achieved a goal.

Ri Armstrong   PHOTO: STEVE STONE

Specifics about the Program follow:

Coverage The Program teaches skiing to the visually- and hearing-impaired; post-polio; single, double, triple and quadruple amputees; spinal cord injured, neurologically impaired; cerebral palsy, multiple sclerosis, muscular dystrophy; spina bifida; arthegriposis; persons with brain aneurisms; the developmentally disabled and emotionally disturbed. These are the major categories of the 45 disabilities covered by the Program.

"The extra effort and patience of your staff keep everyone going in the same direction."

Staff The Program's core staff of five administrative personnel, four equipment room personnel and 13 full-time instructors is supplemented by more than 850 interns and volunteers.

Volunteers Approximately 60,000 volunteer hours are donated each year. See the special section on volunteers for details.

Contract Programs Local programs are by contract with a specific organization, and generally designed to run once a week for eight consecutive weeks. Out-of-state programs are by reservation with the Handicap Program office. These people typically stay a whole week, and the contract is with the sponsoring organization.

Lessons

Roughly 400 lessons are taught each week, seven days a week, to 3,000 skiers each year. In 1986, 13,729 lessons were taught by the 850 volunteers and paid instructors. Virtually all instruction is on a one-to-one basis. Full-time instructors are ready to teach all disabilities; volunteer instructors are trained to teach a specific disability. Individual lessons are offered at 9:00 and 11:30 a.m. and 2:00 p.m. Each lesson is two hours long and by appointment only. The $12.00 lesson charge* covers tow ticket, equipment and individual instruction. Local programs' lessons run from January to the close of season, average eight weeks in duration, running from 9:00 a.m. to 3:00 p.m.

Volunteer Ski Instructors' Training

Training consists of one dry land clinic (orientation, registration) and six on-the-hill clinics. The first three on-the-hill clinics focus on the American Teaching System. The last three pertain directly to the disability with which the instructor will be working. All seven sessions are mandatory in order to be a volunteer instructor.

Professional Certified Ski Instructors

A professional certified ski instructor of the handicapped must be trained in ATS and must also be able to teach the various disabilities (three track, four track, blind, deaf, etc.) and understand the use of adaptive equipment. Certification is through the National Handicapped Sports and Recreation Association. An instructor needs to ski at an advanced (expert) level.

Joe Reum

Cooperation with Ski School

The regular ski school can be very helpful in the area of training in ATS as part of the required certification above, or for certification with Professional Ski Instructors of America. Generally speaking, a ski teaching program for the disabled needs its own teaching group because of the highly specialized adaptive instruction and equipment.

Ski Patrol; Lift Evacuation

Ski patrol needs to be aware of the disabilities with which a handicap program works. They also need instruction in the evacuation of lifts in the event of lift failure for the sit skis and mono-skis, as well as other disabilities.

Accidents

Due largely to the screening and evaluation of the disabled and the extensive training of staff and volunteers working on a one-to-one basis with the individuals, accidents occur very infrequently.

Insurance/ Liability

The Winter Park Sports and Learning Center (the Winter Park Handicap Program's legal name) is fully covered under the insurance of the Winter Park Recreation Association. If your program is not covered by your ski area, insurance may be obtained from the National Handicapped Sports and Recreation Association, provided that your program is a chapter of the national organization.

David Jamison, post polio, International Champion   PHOTO: R.J. WALKER

Racing and Competition

During the season, the Program sponsors a variety of fun races and competitions for Program participants of all ability levels. These events are staged for specific groups as a culmination of their participation. The Winter Park Handicapped Competition Center is covered on page 119.

Program and Equipment Fees

In the past, the Program was able to offer its services at no charge to participants, using contributions and other funding to cover costs. However, due to growing demand

for new and advanced equipment, special technology in adaptive equipment and increases in the number of lessons taught, a Program fee of $12.00* per person per lesson was initiated. A $7.00 fee* is charged for equipment usage without a lesson. These fees cover only a portion of the total lesson cost incurred in running the not-for-profit Program. Tax-deductible contributions are requested from participants who can afford to make additional donations.

Scholarship Fund

A scholarship fund has been set up to assist institutions that do not have the financial capacity to cover fully their clients' participation in the Program. Guidelines and application procedures are handled by the office.

Reduced Lift Tickets

Any handicapped individual who skis at Winter Park but does not use the Program's instruction may purchase a reduced lift ticket at the Handicap Office. Reduced season passes are also available there.

Ski Buddy Tickets

For "ski buddies" who are accompanying a handicapped friend, Winter Park offers a reduced "ski buddy ticket." This ticket must be approved and purchased in the Handicap Office.

Racing and Competitions

During the ski season, the Program sponsors a variety of races and competitions. There is an awards party at the end of the season. Many of the Winter Park handicapped ski racers go on to become part of the National Handicap Ski Team sponsored by the National Handicap Sports and Recreation Association.

Summer Program

For the past 11 years, there has been a very active summer program for the handicapped. Some of the activities are: rafting on the Colorado River, hiking, backpacking, overnight camping, nature walks, alpine slide, chair lift rides, dance movement and adaptive swimming and tennis.

"A summer filled with good memories of rafting and other alpine adventures."

We also offer an extensive rock climbing program for the visually impaired, available for college credit.

*All fee information is subject to change.

Summer rafting is one of the varied activities.

Handicap skiing has many forms — each a specialty in its own right. It may be true that one gave rise to the next, but historically handicap skiing seems to have its roots in two contributing forces: accidental injury and war. While it is risky to try to pinpoint exact beginnings of a sport so tied to world events like war, the earliest information does seem to center in Europe around World War II and focuses on three track.

Through oral accounts given in Europe, the concept of "crutch skiing" originated in Switzerland. The Swiss attempted to utilize underarm crutches for skiing but eventually discarded this technique.

In 1942, a German named Franz Wendel was the first person to successfully enter competition for the handicapped. After a leg amputation from a war injury in 1941, he fashioned a pair of crutches and attached them to short skis, enabling him to begin crutch skiing. By 1943 he was being recognized for his three track skiing. In Austria the sport began to spread by word of mouth. The encouragement and promotion of the sport by those who pioneered it helped others to get started.

By the late 1940's, the Austrian Ski Association was financing a division for the handicapped and in 1947 organized demonstrations by amputee skiers at local annual races.

Concurrently there were European and American personalities involved with rehabilitation programs at army hospitals for amputees. Over these years, various attempts to develop and refine instructional techniques and, more importantly, adaptive equipment, were taking place. By the late 1950's, there was a ski school for amputees in Salzburg, Austria, and the first manuals on the techniques of amputee skiing had begun to appear.

By this time three track skiing had diffused by word of mouth from Europe to the United States. Again, it was the dedication and concern of a small group of people that nurtured and kept alive the developing sport of three track skiing. Some were amputees themselves, some instructors, and at least one or two were specialists in prostheses.

In the early 1960's, this group had acquired several pair of outriggers from an Austrian firm and literally passed them around the country, to copy and refine. The sport traveled westward, developing practitioners in Oregon especially. In the 1962-63 ski season, America had its first certified amputee ski instructor from the United States Ski Association's Northwestern Division. Handicapped skiing was underway in the U.S.A.

With additional outriggers in circulation, amputee ski schools began to flourish in America. By 1962 there was a National Amputee Skiers' Association. (The name was changed to National Inconvenienced Sportsman's Association in 1972.) Today this group has many active chapters in various states in the United States.

Mrs. Virginia McMurtry and Matthew Koldeway.

Teddy Kennedy training for Handicap National Championships at Winter Park.

The Viet Nam War produced regrettable casualties but also provided a boost to the general development of three track skiing. At Fitzsimmons General Hospital near Denver, the need for rehabilitation of amputees, support of their morale, and the presence of nearby magnificent skiing in the Colorado Rockies combined to move three track skiing to the forefront.

In January of 1968, the Children's Amputee Clinic at Denver's Children's Hospital became another contributing force by starting a handicapped ski group. Starting at Arapahoe Basin, the programs soon moved to Winter Park, Colorado, where they have flourished ever since.

Equipment also underwent many changes and refinements over these years, modifying outriggers many times to make them functional. Perhaps the most significant improvement was the development of the flipski. The flipski can be changed from a skiing outrigger into a crutch for walking or climbing by a hand operated lanyard that is connected from the handle to a spring loaded mechanism that locks the ski in either position, as desired.

It has been said that, with the modern adaptive equipment, the special abilities required of a ski instructor for the handicapped are: (1) a technical knowledge of the mechanics of skiing; (2) adequate knowledge of the handicapping condition; and (3) the ability to combine these for maximum efficiency in each unique situation for each individual's benefit. The new outlook that is offered the handicapped through skiing goes beyond increased mobility. It is physical and psychological access to ''normal'' activity.

Today, there are disabled ski associations in ski races and competitions around the world — most notably the Canadian Association for Disabled Skiing, with groups in several provinces and an Annual Canadian International Disabled Ski Meet, and the Handicapped Skiers Association of Japan, with similar competitions annually. Other countries that have programs for handicapped skiers include Norway, France, Italy, Czechoslovakia, Yugoslavia and New Zealand.

From the beginning, when Franz Wendel became the first successful handicapped competitor, competition has been the natural outgrowth of programs. But it was the personal desire for achievement, a love of skiing, and the concern of an international network of dedicated persons that made it all happen.

— A. P. wirephoto
MATTHEW KOLDEWAY, 9, LONGMONT, COLO., WAS ENCOURAGED BY CAPT. RON MORRISON, FORT ATKINSON, WIS.

War, Peace Amputees Learn To Ski on Colorado Slopes

ARAPAHOE BASIN, Colo. — (AP) — Army Capt. Ron Morrison buckled a ski on the one leg he brought back from Vietnam and set off down the snow-swept slope.

A dozen other soldiers, each minus a leg, followed suit. And a like number of children, each gliding on one ski, did likewise.

"It means a lot to get a chance at being people again," said Morrison, 28, Fort Atkinson, Wis., who was wounded twice in Vietnam before a booby trap in the Mekong Delta took his right leg last August 13.

IT WAS AN EFFORT to provide this chance that fostered a learn-to-ski program for Morrison and about 20 other amputees — nearly all Vietnam combat veterans — at the Army's Fitzsimons General Hospital in Denver.

Across town at the same time, Denver Children's Hospital was setting up similar therapy for 18 children who had lost legs either through accident or congenital defect.

Dr. Paul W. Brown, who set up the Fitzsimons program, and Dr. William J. Welnek, who organized it at Children's Hospital, got together and combined their efforts. Now the men and boys make the weekly trip to Arapahoe Basin ski area together.

"I came up here to have a good time. I don't care if I never learn to ski," Morrison said.

But he and his friends are learning.

PROGRESS OF the amputee students has astonished their volunteer instructors at the Willy Schaeffler Ski School.

They figured to keep the amputees on the practice slope for the first four weeks. All were riding the chairlift by the second trip, some made it the first time.

Two soldiers, never on skis until the amputee lessons began, did so well they took their girl friends the next time to teach them.

Most of the amputees were able to navigate a 15-pole slalom race without falling after one or two lessons.

They use an outrigger-type arrangement to stabilize themselves and maintain control. Instead of ski poles, the amputees use poles with very short skis mounted on the ends. Retractable spikes, which can be extended through the stabilizer skis into the snow, are used for walking when the skiers are strapped into their skis.

THE DOUBLE amputees, of course, are skiing without these supporting devices, using skis instead of skates. They can throw away their crutches and be pushed to another activity.

Historical clipping from the collection of Mrs. Virginia McMurtry.

The material in this history was adapted from a research paper, "The History and Development of Three Track Skiing," prepared by Betty Lessard in satisfaction of course work at Michigan State University in June of 1976.

The major trend in three track skiing has been the extension of the use of outriggers to an increasing variety of disabilities. There are now more four trackers than any other type of handicapped skier, and sit skiing is increasing in popularity. Advances in equipment have contributed to this trend.

In 1974 the ski bra was discovered in a ski show. Today the ski bra is standard equipment for the person who does not have control of his legs. But even using the ski bra, some people had trouble in keeping their legs from ''scissoring.'' In 1975 came a device called the toe-spreader — a bar that fits under the bindings and across the skis with ball bearings on either end. In 1976, another development for persons who lacked flex in their lower limbs and knees was the slant board, inserted under the bindings to give a forward or backward slant to the person's stance on the skis. ''Ski legs,'' designed for use by below the knee amputees, are prostheses with the forward lean built into the leg.

Most three trackers agree that the outrigger is most useful for its stability in racing, and in the 1970's the outrigger was refined for speed and efficiency — longer and heavier in the ski tip and shorter in the shaft.

The most radical adaptation of skiing for a disability came in 1978 with the advent of the ''pulk,'' a cross country sled for paraplegics. In 1980 the Arroya, designed for alpine skiing, became a part of the national games. The ''sit ski,'' the Arroya's generic name, has been improved on since.

The growth of handicap skiing in the United States has been reflected in the Handicap Nationals, begun at Winter Park in 1972. In 1978 a freestyle event was added. In 1979 blind skiers were allowed to race alpine, and 1980 saw Arroya competition. Then in 1982 a system of regional qualifiers was adopted in order to manage the greater number of competitors.

Skiers of all abilities may now race in their local chapter or regional race to classify. ''A'' racers go on to the national championships. The highly competitive nature of this regional format promises to field athletes of higher and higher calibre for international competition.

The United States hosted a team to the Second Winter Olympic Games for the disabled in Geilo, Norway in 1980. At the World Games in Switzerland in 1982, for the first time additional categories of disabled skiing were opened to competition, including four track and blind.

Susan Hildebrecht, cerebral palsy, instructor   PHOTO: STEVE STONE

Chris Lind, 1970

Sit skier Marilyn Hamilton
PHOTO: R.J. WALKER

17 | A History. . .Update

Handicap sports catapulted into a new era in 1983 when the International Olympic Committee fully sanctioned the Third World Winter Games for the Disabled. Olympic sanction was a major breakthrough not only in prestige, but it also propelled fundraising efforts and program development worldwide. In October of that same year, a 24 member ''demonstration team'' chosen from selected handicap classifications was invited to participate in a demonstration at the Winter Olympic Games in Sarajevo, Yugoslavia.

"I never had such an experience as the Handicap Nationals. I haven't been so impressed by anything in a long time."

The Third World Winter Disabled Ski Championships were held in 1986 at Salen, Sweden. The United States team, representing a wide and highly capable range of skiing disabled, placed first.

It is apparently the intention of the International Olympic Committee to include demonstrations of handicap competition at the 1988 Winter Games in Calgary, Alberta, Canada. By 1992, it is the intent of the IOC to schedule handicap events as bona fide Olympic medal events.

World Championships in Saalen, Sweden, 1986.   PHOTO: STEVE STONE

Editor's Note   *The Handicap Nationals held at Winter Park between 1972 and 1981 are now moved around the country on a yearly basis. Winter Park will not only host the 1989 Nationals but has also bid on hosting the 1990 World Disabled Ski Championships. This will be the first time these games will be held in North America.*

''Update'' adapted from a paper by Cale Kenney, January, 1983.

*Excerpted by permission of P.S.I.A. Steering Committee from **Strategies for Teaching ATS**, Publishers Press, Salt Lake City, Utah. 1987.*

Beginning Through Wedge Turns

Getting Started

Introduce the student to the mountain environment and safety.
Orient the student to the equipment.
Introduce basic maneuvers: walking, stationary turning, turning while walking, and climbing.

Terrain and Conditions

Begin on the flat.
The ideal beginner area should be well groomed and packed.
For gliding move to a gentle slope.
It is not possible in every ski area but pick terrain that allows the student to ski to a stop.
Match student's skill to the terrain.

Mechanics

Apply the basic skills.
Develop an awareness of controlling pressure in walking and climbing exercises, controlling edging in climbing and gliding wedge exercises, and controlling turning in the gentle gliding wedge turn.
Establish a gliding relationship between skis and snow.
Emphasize skills equally.

Walking

Introduce basic walking steps. When doing self-propelling movements, we suggest that poles be used by adult students but that they not be used for children. Pole swing and position of the basket or end of the pole should be shown in relationship to stride.

Turning Steps

Do turning steps by stepping the tail around (pivot around the tip), then by stepping the tip around (pivot around the tail). Do them in both directions.

Climbing Steps

Begin with a side step. Emphasize the need for the ski to be across the fall line, edging movements, and pressure control movements. Little steps support good edge contact and help maintain balance.

SKILLS APPLICATION

Pressure Control Movements
Emphasize in walking and climbing maneuvers
Edging Movements
Emphasize in climbing maneuvers
Rotary Movements
Emphasize in turning steps, gliding wedge turns, wedge turns
Balancing Movements
Emphasize in the introduction of all basic maneuvers

Gliding Movements Movements for which the primary motive force is external (gravity).

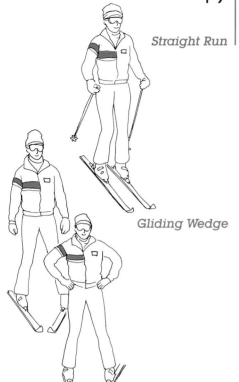

Straight Run | Seek a comfortable position with the feet slightly apart and the joints of the body gently flexed. Students should be able to ski to a comfortable stop. If this is not possible in your area, use a side hill approach instead of a straight downhill run.

Gliding Wedge | From a comfortably high stance (the hips are centered and the body is supported on the skeletal structure rather than by muscular effort) the tails of the skis are pressed slightly apart. The tips are together, and there is litle, if any, edge angle between the ski and the snow. (Those who have little difficulty pressing to a wedge can ski it with the hands relaxed at the side. Others should place the hands on the hips. The ideal situation for students at this stage of development is to be without poles, but if they cannot get back up the hill or need the poles for balance, they should be given to them.)

Wedge Change Ups | This maneuver strengthens the ability to move easily to a comfortable wedge position. From the straight run, the skis are gently brushed into a gliding wedge. After gliding a few feet the skier rises slightly and allows the skis to run together. This exercise should be repeated several times. Initially the student may only be able to go from a straight run to a wedge. With practice the student will be comfortable going from the straight run to the wedge and back again several times.

Gliding Wedge Turns

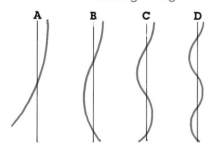

From a straight gliding wedge both skis are gently guided in the direction you wish to go. (No effort is made to edge or pressure the skis.) Both legs are turned in the desired direction of travel. A high body position is maintained with the hips centered. This turn should be kept very close to the fall line and will initially consist of no more than a slight deflection from the original line of travel (A), follow the first turn by gentle deflection out of the fall line in two directions (B), and then link several turns (C). Many instructors find the first gliding wedge is accomplished by simply looking in the desired direction of travel.

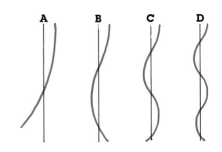

Though we call this a gliding wedge turn, as more belly is added to the turn (D) the components of controlling pressure and edging movements become more pronounced and braking becomes more active in the turn.

Remember that these maneuvers do not have to start in the fall line. Starting at a slight diagonal to the fall line makes the first turn easier to start.

Braking Wedge   The hips are maintained in a central position, but the tails of the skis are brushed out far enough to create significant edge angles between the ski and the snow. This requires greater muscle control than the gliding wedge and should not be practiced until the gliding wedge is mastered or the terrain and conditions require it.

Braking Movements   Movements that counteract natural motive forces to slow down or decelerate (internally generated).

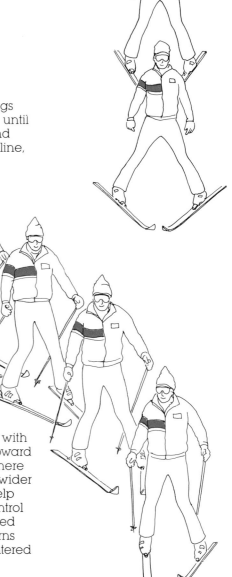

Wedge Turns   From a medium width wedge begin by turning the legs in the desired direction of travel. Keep the skis turning until they have passed beyond the fall line. Edge angle and pressure increases on the ski as the ski crosses the fall line, but this should not be emphasized.

When the skier maintains a comfortably high stance, with hips centered, pressure and edge increase naturally toward the end of the turn. (If you are teaching in an area where the snow is quite hard, you will want to emphasize a wider wedge to provide snow edge relationships that will help control speed.) Side hill approaches to encourage control through application of light pressure on a slightly edged ski can be helpful. Also changing the shape of the turns has an impact on speed control. The hip must stay centered and only come down enough to allow a comfortable wide wedge.

Wedge Turn to Wedge Christy
Introduce the students to and help them become comfortable with the dynamics of skiing (feel the forces generated by a body in motion and begin to work with them).
Strengthen rotary movement skills (directing the skis by controlling turning).
Emphasize two legged steering.
Develop the student's ability to unmatch and match the skis and combine these movements with a wedge turn.
Encourage the match and skid movement at the completion of the turn.

Terrain and Conditions
Select moderate, non-threatening, and packed slopes for your students at this level.
Practice slopes should complement the student's ability.

Mechanics
Rotary movements, edging movements, pressure control movements, and balancing movements are now more interdependent and less independent of each other (they work in combination with each other).
The ability to hold and pressure an edge is beginning at this stage.
The students begin to utilize ski design to assist in developing turn shape.
Unmatching and matching develop along with a feeling for the point at which each should occur.
Two legged steering is much improved.
A feel for the relationship and mix between steering and skidding and gliding and braking is established.
The use of alternating leg action while in motion is developing.

SKILLS APPLICATION

Pressure Control Movements
Encourage by shaping the turns and using maneuvers crossing the fall line

Edging Movements
Continue to work on turn shape and develop awareness of pressure on inside of downhill foot

Rotary Movements
Emphasize turning both feet and turning the inside foot to match the skis

Balancing Movements
Emphasize by varying terrain and introducing more dynamic skiing

The range of application for each skill is expanding and overlapping more with the other skills at this point. The interplay of the skills increases as the student's ability increases.

Wedge Turns With Shape
The student's ability to perform a wedge christy will be influenced by the shape of the turns they are able to do and the speed at which the turns are performed. Start out by using the gliding wedge turn and shape it. Add turns with tighter arcs, encouraging more turn uphill to finish. Put *belly* into the turns. Do turns over terrain that has gentle fall aways and changes in its shape. Under these conditions matching will often happen spontaneously. Introduce turns at slightly higher speeds but keep in mind the ability and comfort zone of your students.

Slipping Wedge Traverse
In a gentle wedge position with the skis pointing across the slope, encourage a high stance with increased pressure on the inside of the downhill foot. Edge engagement should be weak at this point but sufficient to support a slipping traverse. This exercise will teach edge control movements and help students over terrain that may otherwise be too much of a challenge.

Traverse To A Turn
Simply combine the slipping wedge traverse with a wedge turn. This exercise often results in a spontaneous matching. Emphasis is on the turn and its shape with the

traverse as a tool to help the students get from one point to another.

Variations in Wedge Width

Have your students perform turns beginning with wide, medium, and narrow wedge widths. Making adjustments in wedge width and using varying terrain will often result in very relaxed wedge christies without using contrived exercises.

For those who may still be having some problems, emphasize turning or steering the inside leg to facilitate matching. With this active matching movement, encourage a skid after the fall line.

Fall Line Skid Exercises

1 Have your students start in a gliding wedge with the skis pointing into the fall line. Make very short, wiggle like, wedge turns in the fall line. Encourage the pivoting of both skis (braquage) to make the turns.

2 Work at turning both feet in the same direction out of a small wedge.

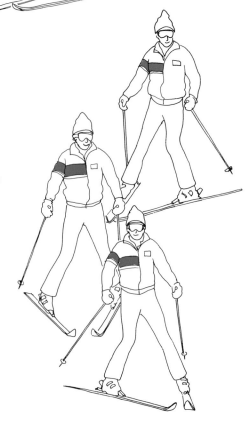

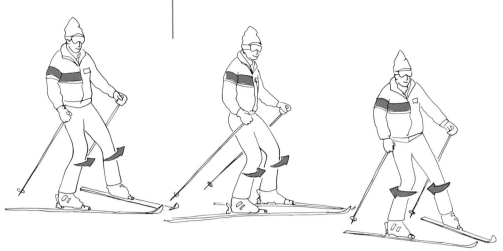

3 Make small wedge garlands across the slope in both directions. Start in a shallow line for the first garlands and then steepen as the students become more proficient with the maneuver. Continue to emphasize turning skills. Remind your students to turn both legs in the desired direction of travel. Actively turning the inside leg encourages matching and results in a christy.

4 Progress to having the students perform two wedge garlands and turn, then two in the other direction and turn, and then have them do one garland and turn. This will induce skidding spontaneously.

5 Have your student do the slipping wedge traverse, introduced earlier as an exercise, and add round turns to it. Continue to develop turning skills and encourage a soft weight transfer followed by a slight sinking to match. Sinking helps maintain balance and supports gentle edging movements.

Vary the terrain the students are skiing on and use a narrow wedge with more turning and skidding on flat terrain. Encourage the use of pressure and edging movements to control speed and direction of travel on steeper terrain.

Wedge Christy | The purpose of the exercises suggested has been to lead the student to a spontaneous wedge christy. Their first turns were characterized by tentative matching and skidding at the very end of the turn. Have your students consciously change the place where the skis are matched. Adjust the matching to coincide with terrain and speed changes. Slow turns on shallow slopes will have a later matching; faster turns on steeper slopes will be characterized by an earlier matching. The uphill christy fan started from a slipping wedge traverse is a good exercise for practicing matching and turn completions.

The wedge christy is intended to lead gently to more efficient turns. An active effort to match the skis and a positive two-footed steering guides students easily to the first wide track parallel turns. The wide track parallel turn is our next objective.

As we progress toward wide track parallel with our students, the objective is to match the skis earlier and earlier in the turn. Figure four shows the beginning of active matching in this illustration. Our goal will be to encourage matching sooner, first in figure three, and then in two until we have a true wide track parallel.

Wide Track To Linked Parallel

Execute turns with the skis in a parallel relationship.
Emphasize the development of rotary movement skills.
Link parallel turns; emphasize turning with rhythm.
Begin to explore the range of edging and pressure control movements and their relationship to turn shapes.
Help the student relate to the movements and feelings associated with the initiation and finish of the turn.

Perform turns with a variety of turn shapes.

Terrain

Continue to ski gentle terrain. On gentle terrain the student can stay closer to the fall line, making it easier to start each turn. Your students should be able to link turns without fear of gaining too much speed.

Terrain selection is either a help or a hindrance to skiers. As skill level improves, steeper and more difficult terrain can be used to enhance growth in ability. More difficult terrain should not be introduced at the same time new movement patterns are being taught.

Mechanics

At this level, the wedge is no longer the only platform from which maneuvers are initiated. Movements that enhance skills application are now part of the students' performance pool. Turns are characterized by a slight up movement to release edge at the initiation and a flexing to increase edge angle through the turn. Rotary movements guide the skis through the turn and lead to a simple edge engagement as the turn is completed.

A subtle weight transfer is applied at this stage of skiing. Rotary movements, pressure control movements, and edging movements are also becoming more refined.

SKILLS APPLICATION

Pressure Control Movements
Edging Movements
Rotary Movements
Balancing Movements

At this level of skiing the basic skills not only overlap but support one another in application. Exercise lines are used to assist students in strengthening their use of the skills. The instructor's job is to use exercises to accomplish an objective, e.g., skating to enhance pressure control movements, edging movements, and balancing movements.

Wide Track Parallel

Some students spontaneously progress from a wedge christy into wide track parallel without going through build-up exercises. For such individuals the following sequence of exercises should be used to strengthen the skills they have already developed. Others need these and additional exercises to do their first parallel turns.

*Christy Fan
or
Uphill Christy*

Begin in a high stance doing a shallow slipping traverse. Sink down and turn both legs (skis) up hill and christy to a stop. Repeat this exercise several times to get the feeling of two legged turning from a parallel position.

After success with this maneuver from a shallow traverse move progressively nearer to the fall line with your start. Now begin at a point where you will have to cross the fall line slightly in order to finish in the same direction as in the first turns.

Increase speed and seek greater change in direction. Emphasize turning both legs in the desired direction of travel.

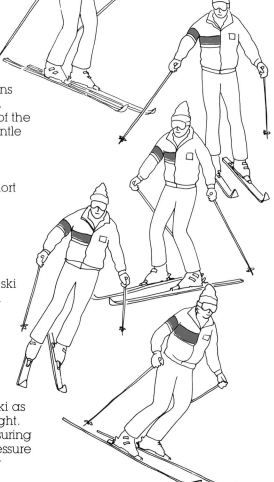

Fall Line Wide Track Turns

On a gentle slope start in a high stance. Make foot turns (think of turning the feet only) just crossing the fall line. Make the same shape turns but feel the involvement of the feet and knees. Make the turns rhythmical using a gentle up to start and a down to continue the christy action. Add rhythm turns with slight up and down motion.

Now smooth movements out and you have a good short radius wide track turn.

Wide Track Turns With Weight Transfer

Begin either from a side track or a wedge position.

From the fall line, slightly flex down and turn the right ski as you pick up on (take pressure off of) the left ski and gently turn it to the left. (You will turn left.)

From the fall line, slightly flex down and turn the left ski as you pick up on the right ski and gently turn it to the right. You will turn right. (You may emphasize flexing and pressuring the outside ski of the turn. We have talked of taking pressure off of the inside ski because it decreases the tendency to turn the hips in the direction of the desired turn.)

Repeat the moves already practiced emphasizing flexing of the joints over the weighted ski and rhythmically move from one turn to another.

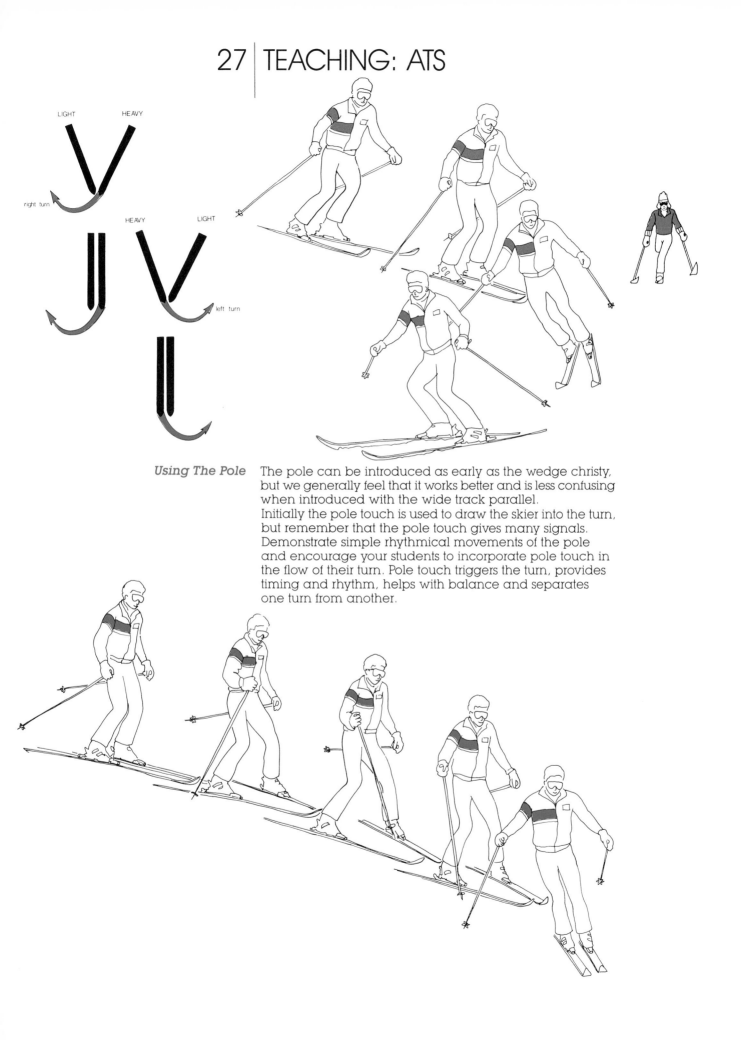

LIGHT HEAVY

right turn

HEAVY LIGHT

left turn

Using The Pole The pole can be introduced as early as the wedge christy, but we generally feel that it works better and is less confusing when introduced with the wide track parallel.

Initially the pole touch is used to draw the skier into the turn, but remember that the pole touch gives many signals. Demonstrate simple rhythmical movements of the pole and encourage your students to incorporate pole touch in the flow of their turn. Pole touch triggers the turn, provides timing and rhythm, helps with balance and separates one turn from another.

Wide Track To Linked Parallel

In the last section, we talked about terrain as a variable that can be used to help the student learn. Speed is also a variable that you can use to create different learning situations for the students. Begin slowly, especially in the exercises that do not cross the fall line or are not complete turns like the fan christy. To encourage a parallel relationship go just a little faster. Choose enough speed to make the turn easy without causing the skier to regress because of fear.

Have the students flex and face downhill a little more when performing the fan christy with more speed and as a more complete turn. This encourages a sound basic position through the finish of these low-phase turns. Proper flexing in the ankles and knees is important because some students will bend only in the hips and waist and end up sitting back, thus losing the ability to turn or steer the feet.

Flexing throughout the turn to aid the christy places the skiers in a situation where they must rise to start the skis into the next turn. At this stage the rising action is somewhat vertical (straight up). With increased skill and additional speed, angulation and inclination increase to offset the forces generated in the turn. We are then concerned that the ''up'' moves the skier in the direction of the next turn. For now, it is enough to be moving up and out or down and in enough to give the skier a rhythm and aid in the action of turning and *turning with both feet*.

Turns require different amounts of energy and effort. To learn wide track christies, take the skis off (on flat or very gentle terrain). While balancing against the poles, twist the feet (boots) from side to side. Use a flexing action up and down to help. Also try jumping up and turning the feet (boots) and then landing. (This energetic and athletic movement is fun but not meant for every student.)

Now put the skis back on and on very gentle terrain, continue the feeling of foot turns by gently turning one way and then the other. It should feel like the slight direction changes accomplished are a result of what happens in the feet. Now with flexing in the knees and ankles, enhance rotary movements by directing the knees along with the feet. The whole leg develops turning power, but the focus is guided first to the feet and then to the knees in this exercise. These turns must be done on gentle terrain and must be practiced over and over so the students are comfortable with them.

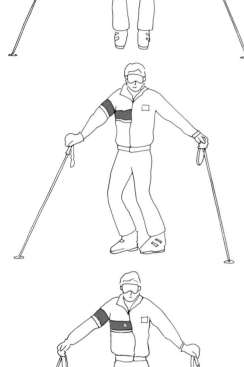

Moving the wide track parallel skier toward more accomplished skiing can be done in several ways. You might simply refine edge and pressure control skills and start moving to longer, more controlled turns. If that works, it's great! If not, here are a few other exercises to try.

Wide track skiers are still accustomed to skiing gentle terrain in the fall line. Show the skiers how to flex down and up, getting the skis off the snow. (This is best suited to athletic students.) Work from an excessive range of motion to the minimum amount of motion needed to cause the skis to come off of the snow. This may first be tried statically and then in motion with slight turns. Work toward making turns across the fall line. The students will realize the turning power that is available to them and gain confidence in their ability to turn for control at any time and still remain in a parallel stance. Rhythm and motion are effective elements that skiers can always draw from. Because we can't hop all day, however, our efforts must be to gradually tone down the unweighting to the point that skiers can maintain strong turns with rhythm without so much up and down.

Use fall line pedal turns for skiers who are just getting started and for the top skier as well. Learning to ski from ski to ski can be a real help to all of us. This exercise can be done in the wedge, but for a skier wishing to evolve with the parallel wide track, a pedal or step turn enhances the ability to remain parallel. The uphill ski is the ski that the skier stands on to start the turn, thereby making it very difficult to stem or wedge. Don't worry about a slight wedge. A slight opening of the tips and tails of the skis is very acceptable as long as it doesn't impede the turn in any way. Stay close to the fall line and the turn is easier. To turn left, pick up the left ski and turn with both knees and feet (legs); to turn right, pick up the right ski and turn both knees and feet to the right. Start slow and gradually develop more speed, rhythm, and turn completion. When you pick up the ski, pick the entire ski slightly off the snow — not the tail only or the tip only.

The three track method is used by individuals who have one good leg and two arms. This technique is adapted from the American Teaching System.

Evaluation

When you are first introduced to your student you will need to find out how severe the handicap is and what kind of adaptive equipment she may need. The evaluation is intended to find the best way for the student to stand on her ski, be comfortable and maintain balance. Usually this requires both special equipment and an individualized technique.

Following are guidelines for the evaluation:

Disabilities Utilizing the Three Track Method	Adaptive Equipment
Above the knee amputees	One ski and two outriggers
Below the knee amputees (with less than 4″ stump)	Same
Double amputee with above the knee amputation and below the knee with more than 4″ stump	Prosthesis, one ski, two outriggers
Post polio	One ski and two outriggers
Trauma	Same
Hemipelvectomy	Same
Hip disarticulation	Same
Individuals with one arm and one leg	One ski and one outrigger

Fitting the Ski

The length of the ski is determined by the height and weight of the student. The ski should be slightly longer than if the individual were skiing on two skis, and should be lengthened according to the student's progress.

It is frequently necessary to cant the ski for a three tracker in order to make the ski flat.

Fitting Outriggers

There is a variety of ways of measuring and fitting outriggers for a beginner. The grip should be placed next to the hip joint when standing (flipski in the down position, clearing the surface by one inch). The cuff should be halfway between the elbow and wrist with the opening pointing outward. Adjust the brake accordingly. As the student progresses, her leg becomes the principal weight bearer and the outrigger is shortened accordingly.

Protecting the Stump

Because circulation is often poor in the stump, it should be covered with a wool stump sock and padding to protect against the cold and falls. This is of the utmost importance. It the student has problems with a cold stump, it can be moved rapidly to increase blood circulation. Make sure hemipelvectomies and hip disarticulations take extra precaution in padding the affected areas.

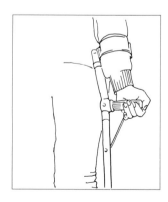

Activate the flipski by pulling up on cord. To depress flipski, pull up on cord again, press down on tail of outrigger's ski.

Walking Without Skis

Flat Terrain, Flipskis Up

Flipskis Down Place flipskis at 45° angle to the boot. Push on the inside edge of both outriggers, hop foot forward, use outriggers in a slight rotary motion.

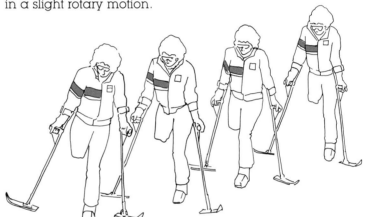

Getting Into Ski Now that the student has been properly fitted, demonstrate how to get into the ski. Put all the weight on the outriggers and lift yourself up over the ski, positioning the toe of the boot in the toe of the binding, the heel in the heel of the binding and push down.

Body Position | Correct body position has flex in the ankle, knee and hip, creating center of gravity and balance from the ball of the foot.

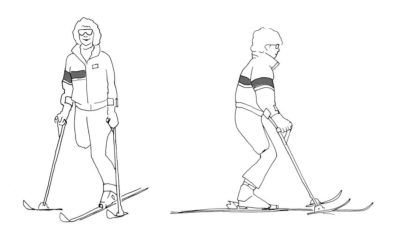

Learn how to walk with flipskis in the down position. Bring the flipski down to walk. Place at a 45° angle to the boot. Push on the inside edge of both outriggers and glide the ski.

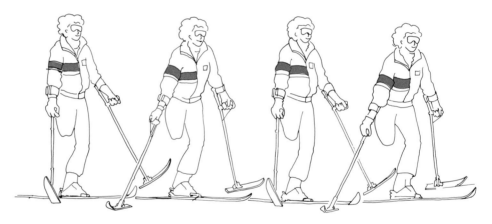

When walking with the flipski up, do not rotate the arms. Push and glide as you would with the ski in the down position.

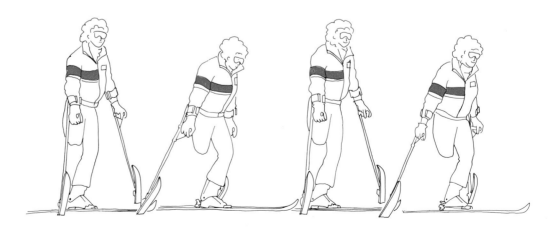

Hop Turn, Flat Terrain At this point the hop turn is taught only as a means of changing direction while in a static position. This will assist the student in developing rhythm and balance as well as in familiarizing himself with the arm-foot coordination needed to use the outriggers. This is a confidence building stage so pace the activity according to the individual's ability. Later the hopping skills will be used to initiate turns once the student is introduced to the traverse maneuver. Please note that this maneuver can be performed with the flipski in either the up or down position.

To Fall When teaching the student to fall, show her how to lower the body holding the stump in with the outriggers up and outward, making sure the chin is tucked inward while falling in order to protect the head.

To Get Up A beginner will find it is easier to get up when the stump is positioned uphill. Have her put the outriggers in the walking position, push against the downhill outrigger, remove the uphill outrigger and lean against it, and bring her body over the ski and push herself up.

It is very important that the stump be held tightly against the leg during all maneuvers and to protect it in a fall.

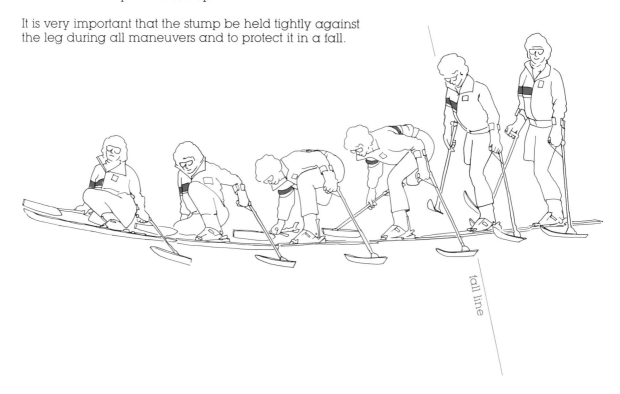

fall line

Climbing, Gentle Terrain

Side stepping is a way of climbing up terrain. What the student should learn is edge control and balance. The stump should be on the uphill side, held tightly against the body. Place the ski across the fall line. With a slight forward and uphill motion, hop the ski uphill. Stress edge control to your student. Use hop turns to get into the fall line.

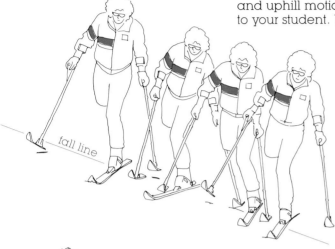

Straight Run

Straight run position: outriggers flipped down comfortably between the tip of the ski and the toe of the boot, shoulder width apart, knee bent, slightly flexed at the waist, body weight on the leg. Let the ski go.

To Stop

Use the outriggers as brakes, lower the elbows to the hips and push into the bottom of the outriggers.

When working on the straight run, the terrain should be gentle. It is important that most of the body weight be carried by the leg. When the student has accomplished the straight run to a stop, she is ready for the chair lift.

Loading the Chair Lift

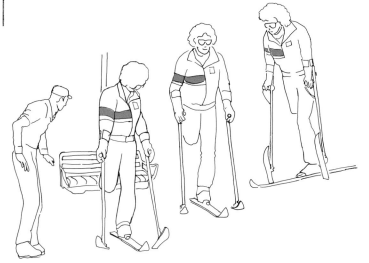

In loading the chair lift, have your student watch how other people load. Move into the loading area, flip the outriggers in the down position, look to the inside and sit down. Student must lift outriggers off the ground as she sits.

An important note to remember when loading the chair: The flipski should be down to prevent breaking the outriggers and injury to the upper body. For safety reasons, the outrigger should never be removed while riding the chair lift.

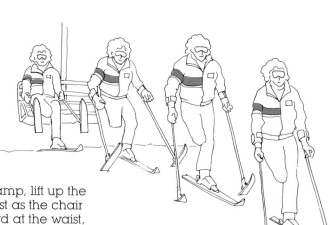

Unloading the Chair Lift

As the chair approaches the unloading ramp, lift up the tip of the ski and the outriggers. Unload just as the chair reaches the unloading ramp. Lean forward at the waist, bend the knee and stand up.

Ski down the ramp by assuming the straight running position.

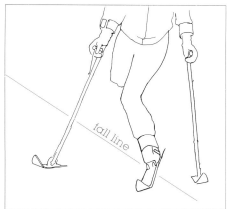

...se gentle wide terrain. This maneuver will require ...teral movement of the knee and ankle into the hill to maintain the edge of the ski. As the student crosses the slope, the outriggers are held shoulder width apart; the ankle, knee and upper body are slightly flexed. Use the tail of the outriggers to stop. Use hop turns to take a new direction. Repeat this maneuver several times in both directions.

Exercise: Brake and turn using outriggers to slow, leaving the ski easy to pivot in preparation for the uphill christie; for students who fear the fall line.

After the student has become familiar with the traverse maneuver, introduce steering the foot into the hill, with a slight heel displacement to help turn the ski, then releasing the pressure and flattening the ski, letting it drift toward the fall line, continuing to steer the ski into the hill as before. This creates garlands and can be used as an exercise to prepare the student for turns.

A garland is a series of scallop-like figures carved across the fall line, as demonstrated above.

Uphill Christie

The uphill christie will get your student accustomed to the controlled skid as well as coming to a complete stop. From a traverse the skier begins the uphill christie by flexing the knee forward, followed immediately by a down motion. This releases the edges of the ski and outriggers, allowing them to slip. Steer the ski in the direction of the turn to a stop.

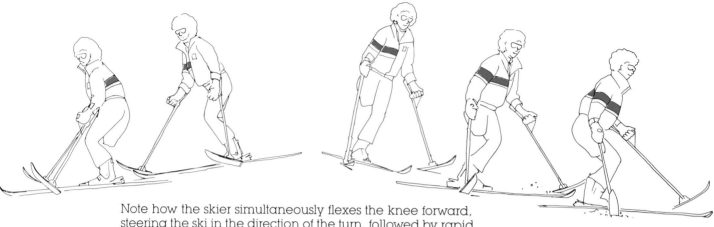

Note how the skier simultaneously flexes the knee forward, steering the ski in the direction of the turn, followed by rapid down movement. Practice this maneuver, moving to moderate terrain and on to the beginning turn.

Beginning Turns

The beginning turns for a three tracker should be performed moving slightly in and out of the fall line by using a relatively flat ski, emphasizing the steering of the foot and displacement of the heel. This will prevent overuse of the ski edge as so many beginners often do in attempting beginning turns. Avoid using the knee to steer.

As the skier progresses, she should be instructed to make the arc of the turn more pronounced. This will encourage the skidding of the ski and in turn assist in control. The student is now ready for advanced christie turns.

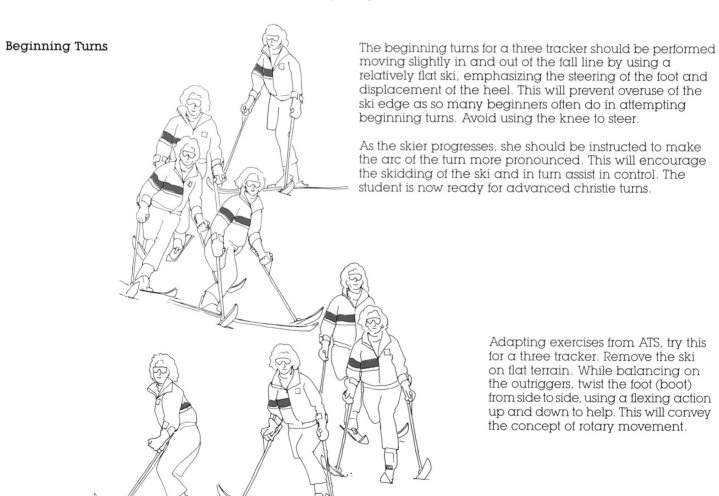

Adapting exercises from ATS, try this for a three tracker. Remove the ski on flat terrain. While balancing on the outriggers, twist the foot (boot) from side to side, using a flexing action up and down to help. This will convey the concept of rotary movement.

Exercise: Outrigger "Pole Plant"

Utilizing the outrigger as a pole, touch the outrigger (flipski down) lightly on the snow, lifting the other outrigger off the snow. Complete turn and repeat. This establishes rhythm and edge control and will lead to an alternating outrigger action.

Advanced Parallel Turns

The student is also ready for more difficult terrain in order to maintain a consistent speed. The arc of the turn should become more pronounced, utilizing the edge to rebound from. This action will carry the skier smoothly from turn to turn. Perfecting this maneuver will enable the skier to move on to the short swing.

Short Swing

Short swinging is a series of successive short radius parallel christies with the traverse between turns eliminated. It is the distinct edge set of each turn that makes this maneuver effective in steep terrain.

Think of the leg and ski as being a pendulum moving in rhythm. The upper body stays centered over the fall line while the leg moves side to side. This motion will perform edge change, rhythm and control. It can lead the skier into the next phase: mogul skiing.

fall line

Moguls After mastering short swing, the student is now a sufficiently advanced and competent skier to undertake mogul skiing, powder skiing and racing.

You will find that individuals who ski three track tend to advance very rapidly. However, it is important to permit the student to progress at a speed that is comfortable to her. The three track method has no limitations. Individuals with a desire to learn can excel in all areas of skiing.

Balancing skills at high speeds: tuck.

Arm Amputees

The American Teaching System applies in teaching arm amputees to ski. However, the following can assist in teaching this type of disability.

Adaptive Equipment

If the student is wearing a prosthesis, the hook should be protected in order to prevent injury and cold while skiing. A heavy leather mitten or even a cork will do.

If the student is an above-the-elbow amputee, it is advised that the prosthesis not be worn while skiing for his own safety. The stump should be protected by a stump sock or other warm material to prevent frostbite.

For the below-the-elbow amputee, it has not proven to be successful to attach a ski pole to the prosthetic side. (It should be mentioned that arm amputees on the Disabled National Team use only one pole while skiing.)

Teaching Tips

Since the amputation of an arm can cause lateral balance problems, it is of the utmost importance when working with an individual without a prosthesis that emphasis be placed on working with the feet and legs. Use simultaneous steering with the feet and legs. Frequently you will find that if this is not emphasized, rotation of the shoulders will cause balance problems.

A pole can be introduced in the very beginning to assist in walking and eventually for pole planting, to create rhythm and to help with edge change and weight shift. To compensate for the absence of an arm, it can be of great assistance if the skier imagines that the arm is still there and, through his mind, creates a pole planting maneuver on the amputated side. This will enable him to make equal arcs in either direction.

It should be left up to the individual whether or not he wears his prosthesis and uses a ski pole.

Bill Dean, former National Champion and coach.　　　PHOTO: R.J. WALKER

Symes Amputation

A Symes amputation is an amputation of the foot at the ankle joint. This presents special problems in fitting the prosthesis into the boot with proper alignment.

Adaptive Equipment

Most individuals with a Symes amputation can be successfully taught to ski on two skis. Because of stump problems, a few ski three track. The American Teaching System applies, with a few adaptations.

Teaching Tips

Emphasis should be placed on the simultaneous steering of both feet and legs. In the beginning, if lateral control continues to be a problem, a ski bra may be used temporarily.

It is advisable that the student begin on a shorter ski and graduate to a longer ski, according to his ability.

Joe Reum, 1975　　　PHOTO: S. COLEMAN

Lower Limb Prosthetics

A person who has had an amputation of his leg and uses a prosthesis must have a comfortable, functional and an acceptable appearing limb replacement to enjoy activities of daily living. Routine tasks can be extremely challenging to complete when performed on one leg or on a prosthesis that causes pain with each step.

Adaptive Equipment

Those involved in teaching amputee skiing will find it helpful to understand a little of lower extremity prosthetics, especially when the student skis with the prosthesis. Just as we know that the relationship between foot-boot-binding-ski is crucial to effect efficient transmission of forces to the snow, so it is between amputation stump and prosthesis. And, just as a ski boot that is either too loose or too tight can be painful and result in blisters or affect blood circulation, so can an ill-fitting prosthesis cause similar conditions and worse.

The situations that affect comfort, function, and ultimately the quality of the skiing experience, are extremely complex: the physical condition of the individual (overall condition and capabilities, and specific conditions relating to the amputation), available technology, the prosthetist's skill and desire to innovate, and the amputee's aspirations and will.

Many single below-the-knee amputee skiers use specially designed prostheses which would mean building the limb with approximately 15 to 21 degrees of forward lean from the ankle with the foot set in a barefoot position. Additional suspension is gained with the attachment of a ''thigh-lacer.'' The thigh-lacer also adds a great deal of stability in a lateral sense, preventing the leg from twisting sideways under the forces of skiing.

It is not necessary to have a ''ski leg'' in order to get started. A standard walking leg can be used with some simple modifications. A tight elastic sleeve pulled up over the knee and thigh will greatly stabilize stump pistoning and rotation. If the walking leg is set up for an average walking shoe, you can make a wedge of 2 to 5 cm. to give the proper forward lean inside the ski boot. If you do this, it will be necessary to add a flat lift under the binding of the good leg in order to keep the hips level.

Often the prosthetic limb will also have to be aligned so the knee is located in line with the hip and ankle when viewed from the front of the skier. These are the basic adjustments for a skier in a single or double below-the-knee situation.

"Jill, now 13 and an above-the-knee amputee, had never skied before her amputation. With your lessons and equipment, she is as good as the rest of us and skiing is something we can do together."

The four track method of skiing is so named because the skier is actually relying on four separate ski sources to navigate the ski slope. This method allows the skier to equalize weight on both legs by using two normal, full-sized skis. To achieve extra additional balance, the four track skier uses two outriggers. Four tracking is often used when instructing people with aneurisms, cerebral palsy, post polio, spina bifida, arthrogryposis, muscular dystrophy or multiple sclerosis and those who suffer from a congenital defect or traumatic accident, as well as others.

The ski bra or bungi cord is often used in four track skiing.

Evaluation Four tracking has become a popular system of skiing because it is so adaptable to a variety of disabilities. An individual who has two arms and two legs, natural or prosthetic, and is capable of standing, is a candidate for the four track method. Sometimes a combination of adaptive equipment is required.

Individuals Utilizing the Four Track Method	Adaptive Equipment: Outriggers Plus
Those with lack of lateral control	Ski bra or bungi cord
Inability to walk without assistance of crutches, cane, etc.	Same
Tendency to fall forward, walk on toes or lean heavily on crutches or walker	Slant board with toe raised*
Pronounced backward lean	Slant board with heel raised (if moderately involved, heel lifts not exceeding 1″ under bladder in boot)

*When toe raises are used, the outriggers should be lengthened accordingly.

The ski bra gives more control to the feet, legs and hips and helps maintain a parallel position while skiing. It consists of two metal devices that are slipped over and affixed to each ski tip. One metal piece is an eyelet and the other a hook. The ski tip with the hook is latched onto the ski with the eyelet. Although the devices are hooked together, the ski bra allows the skier flexibility of movement and a constant position of the skis, which are kept three to four inches apart.

Consideration of the length of the skis is very important. The length can vary dramatically according to the disability. If the student is extremely weak, a shorter ski should be considered. Students utilizing the slant board with toe lifts or heel raises frequently require longer skis in order to prevent them from overturning.

When first paired with your student, you will evaluate what his needs are and what kind of handicap you are dealing with. As an instructor, your evaluation helps to pinpoint the best way for the student to stand on his skis, be comfortable and maintain his balance. In evaluating a four tracker, there are three positions you will work with: normal, leaning back and leaning forward. The aim of the evaluation is to create adaptive equipment to bring the individual to a balanced position. For the individual who leans forward, a slant board can be utilized to raise the toes, creating a balanced position. If the individual leans backward, then it is necessary to raise the heels. If the individual lacks lateral control of the feet and legs, some sort of a stabilizer must be used: a ski bra for the severely involved and a bungi cord for the lesser involved.

Activating Flipski (see page 30 of Three Track for details)

Review the equipment with your student. Explain how the outriggers work. Describe the ski by pointing out the tip, tail, edges, bindings and their use. Assist your student to find his balance and proper body position. The outriggers should be held shoulder width apart, just forward of the ski boots. They should be used only for balance with most of the weight carried by the legs. Demonstrate how to brake by lowering the elbows and applying pressure on the outriggers.

Getting Into Equipment

Body Position

To establish proper body position, use the touch system in the areas of flex; hip, knee and ankle.

Moving on the Flat

Outriggers Down

Place the outriggers shoulder width apart, even with the heel of the ski boot. Turn the tips out at a 45° angle. Flex the knee. Using the inside edges of the outriggers, push off with the arms, following through with a backward thrust. Finish with the body upright in a position to repeat the maneuver.

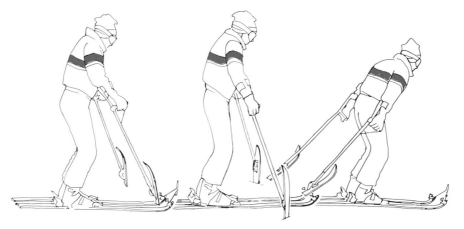

Outriggers Up

Moving Assisted: Two Point Hold

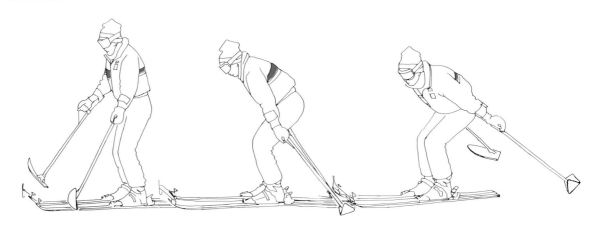

Side Stepping

If the student does not have his ski tips stabilized and is capable of side stepping, move to a gentle slope that has a flat outrun. This is generally not possible with students in the forward or leaning back position.

With the student facing you, explain and demonstrate how the edge is dug in to hold against the hill. If your student is fearful, side step just below him. This will also allow you to help with positioning.

Falling

The four tracker learns to fall the same way as the three tracker, keeping the outriggers clear of the body. See illustration on page 34.

Getting Up: Method #1 — Assisted

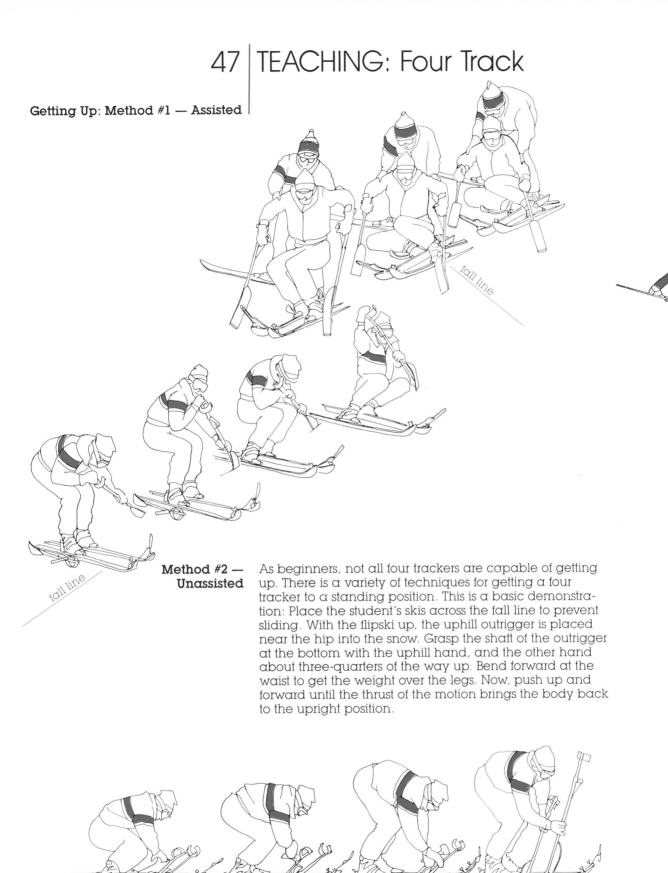

Method #2 — Unassisted

As beginners, not all four trackers are capable of getting up. There is a variety of techniques for getting a four tracker to a standing position. This is a basic demonstration: Place the student's skis across the fall line to prevent sliding. With the flipski up, the uphill outrigger is placed near the hip into the snow. Grasp the shaft of the outrigger at the bottom with the uphill hand, and the other hand about three-quarters of the way up. Bend forward at the waist to get the weight over the legs. Now, push up and forward until the thrust of the motion brings the body back to the upright position.

Method #3 — Unassisted

Walk the hands in a quarter circle from uphill to just over the skis while pushing upward to a standing position with body weight forward from the waist. Sometimes it is easier for the student to get up if you unhook the ski bra.

48 | TEACHING: Four Track

Straight Run

Gentle Terrain, Assisted

Whether a chair lift or the side step is used to move up the hill, the first maneuver is the straight run. In teaching the straight run you will find there is a variety of ways to stabilize the student. This varies according to the severity of the disability. The following demonstrations are two of the most common: Stabilize the student by placing one hand on the tip of the skis and the other on the downhill knee. Slowly move the student into the fall line.

Unassisted Straight Run to a Stop

When dealing with severely involved individuals the two point hold position is utilized for additional stability. There are two ways of performing the two point hold position. The instructor places both hands on the hip or, if the student requires additional stabilization, one hand is positioned on the hip and the other hand just below the opposite knee of the student.

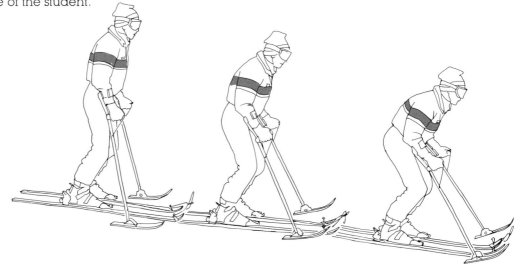

Loading Chair Lift | Introduce the chair lift by watching others, explaining how they load the lift. When your student has an understanding, move into the line and prepare to load. If the outriggers have a flipski, be sure it is in the down position.

Move to the loading position, have the chair slowed, and when the chair is about to make contact, give the command to sit.

While riding the chair lift, explain how to unload. As the unloading area approaches, give the signal to have the chair lift slowed. The widely accepted motion to the lift operator for slowing down is a quick downward motion with the hand, repeated as necessary. To motion to stop the chair, use a horizontal cutting motion across the neck.

Unloading Chair Lift | The student should hold the outriggers out in front with the flipski in the down position. When the skis make contact with the snow, have the student begin to rise up, bending forward at the waist, placing the outriggers on the snow. Ski down the ramp by assuming the straight running position. Move quickly away from the unloading zone.

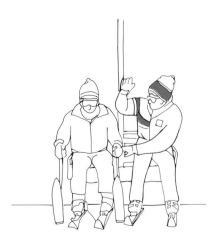

Beginning Turns

(2)

(1)

(3)

(4)

(1)

Phases of a Turn
(1) Preparation
(2) Initiation
(3) Controlling
(4) Finishing
(Credit: ATS Teaching Strategies)

Determine the student's ability to find his center of gravity while moving. This will tell you if the adaptive equipment selected is correct or if further adaptation is needed.

Utilize the two point hold position by placing one hand on the hip and the other hand just below the opposite knee. The instructor should assist and encourage the student with his first turn. Make sure that the student rotates his hips in order to steer the feet and skis in the direction of the turn. Repeat this several times in both directions until the student can accomplish this maneuver without assistance; then move on to steeper terrain and beginning parallel turns. This assumes that the student is unable to steer his feet and knees. If he is able, then work first with that ability.

Using a relatively flat ski, emphasize the rotation of the hips and the steering of both feet and knees in the direction of the turn. The instructor skis backwards, facing the student, and with commands and hand signals, directs the timing and arc of the student's turns. This maneuver should be repeated often enough for the student to become familiar with the phases of a turn.

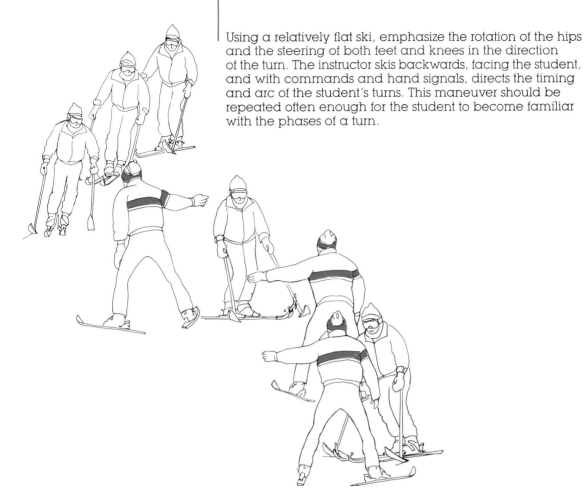

Uphill Christie Exercise From a traverse, have the student initiate a downward movement, steering both skis slightly into the hill to create garlands. Repeat in both directions.

**Linked
Parallel Turns**

As the student progresses with parallel turns, he should be taught to make his turns more pronounced. In so doing, you will find that the student will begin to slide the tails of the skis, quickly setting the edge, resulting in a rebound which will assist the skier in equalizing the arc of each turn, creating timing, rhythm and control.

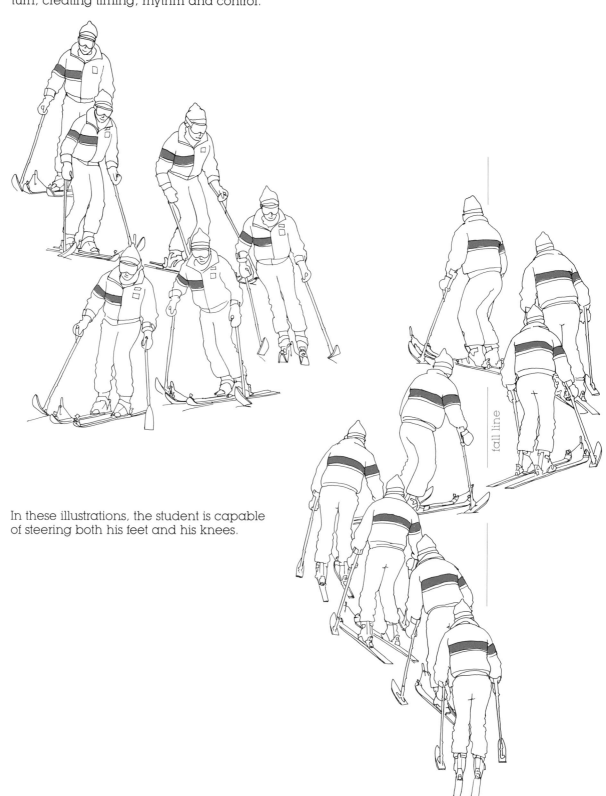

In these illustrations, the student is capable of steering both his feet and his knees.

53 | TEACHING: Four Track

In this illustration, the student is limited to using his hips and above to initiate the turn.

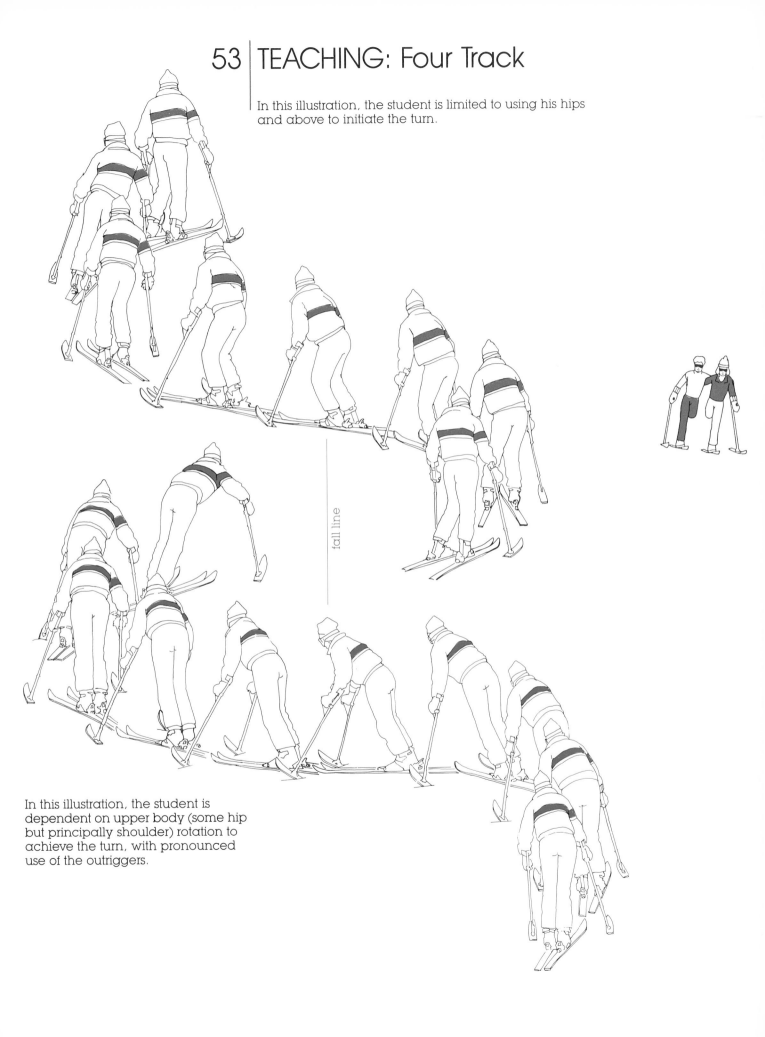

fall line

In this illustration, the student is dependent on upper body (some hip but principally shoulder) rotation to achieve the turn, with pronounced use of the outriggers.

**Advanced
Parallel Turns**

fall line

Short Swing
Short swinging is a series of successive short radius parallel christies with the traverse between turns eliminated. It is the distinct edge set of each turn that makes this maneuver effective in steep terrain.

Think of the legs and skis as being a pendulum moving in rhythm. The upper body stays centered over the fall line while the legs move side to side. This motion will perfect edge change, rhythm and control. It can lead the skier into the next phase: mogul skiing.

**Moguls
Racing**
After mastering short swing, the student is now a sufficiently advanced and competent skier to undertake mogul skiing, powder skiing and racing.

Because skiers advance at different speeds, the technique could take days or months to accomplish. Remember: Skiing is not for everyone. But for those who want to learn, it enhances their freedom of movement and feeling of independence.

Four Track With Monoboard

Monoboard skiing is used for individuals who do not have or cannot risk independent leg action. It is a specialized form of four track. People for whom the monoboard might be indicated include: severe hip problems; individuals with full leg braces; individuals with high bi-lateral amputations utilizing their prostheses.

Beth Fox, instructor, on monoboard.
PHOTO: JEANNE SMITH

"He sometimes gets up at 1:00 a.m. on ski days because he's too excited to sleep. Other times he goes to bed at 6:00 p.m. the night before ski days, to make sure he is rested up for skiing!"

Cerebral palsy has many different forms. This section concentrates on hemiplegia — involvement of one side. Other forms include: quadraplegia and diaplegia. The basic instruction that follows can be adapted to the individual case utilizing ATS wherever possible.

Evaluation

When introduced to your student, you will evaluate his special needs. Cerebral palsy affects the brain, causing balance and coordination problems. For a beginning skier, it is the most difficult of all disabilities to work with. Its effects can range from slight to severe impairment of mobility. During the initial evaluation you will find that no two individuals are alike. Equipment as well as technique must be modified for each person. In some cases, a combination of adaptive equipment is required.

"While her cerebral palsy prevents her from walking without assistance, you refused to allow it to prevent her from skiing."

Effects of Cerebral Palsy	Adaptive Equipment
Difference in leg length	Heel lift placed underneath bladder in boot or binding or slant board in severe cases.
Lack of lateral control	Ski bra or bungi cord
Inability to walk without assistance of crutches, cane, wheelchair, etc.	Outriggers (for those capable of grasping). In some instances instead of outriggers, a walker with skis attached or, as an alternative, a sit ski is used.
Tendency to fall forward, walk on toes or lean heavily on crutches or walker	Slant board with toe raised (degree varies according to the severity of cord restriction)
Pronounced backward lean	Slant board with heel raised
Scissor gait	Toe bar with or without heel spreader

Teaching Tip: Avoid any abrupt physical contact (e.g., a sudden slap on the back) or loud commands. A surprised reaction from the student could momentarily disorient him or even cause him to lose his balance.

Do not use ski poles in the beginning. The reason is that people with cerebral palsy have a tendency to overgrip. As the student progresses, poles can be introduced. Use a ski bra in the beginning to stabilize the tips of the skis. Doing so will stabilize the legs and hips. Depending on the severity of the student's involvement, a bungi cord may be substituted for the ski bra. A lift is used to correct a leg length difference. In most cases, 135 cm skis are used for all beginners. However, it does vary according to the height, weight and ability of the individual.

If the student is unable to maintain a proper position, a slant board can be utilized to correct the position by raising the toes or heels according to the needs of the individual.

If the student's balance is marginal and he is capable of grasping outriggers, a modified Canadian crutch with a ski tip should be used.

Getting Into Equipment   Begin your lessons by familiarizing your student with the equipment. Explain the parts of the ski. Demonstrate how to enter and exit the bindings. Have your student try it without assistance.

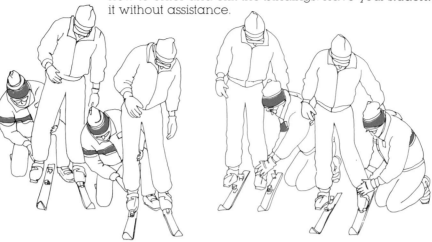

In assisting a hemiplegic with getting into his equipment, start with his strong side.

Body Position   Once your student is in the equipment, help him find his balance. Demonstrate the proper body position. While on flat terrain, have your student get used to his new feet by moving around a little. Watch him carefully for signs of fatigue.

To establish proper body position, use the touch system in the areas of flex: hip, knee and ankle. To keep the weak arm from flailing, teach the student to grasp the edge of the parka or to put it in his pocket.

Side Stepping   During the warmup determine if your student is capable of side stepping or whether the chair lift must be used to find a gentle slope. If your student is able to side step, move to a terrain that has a slight incline and a sufficiently flat outrun.

If the student has difficulty in side stepping, place his strong side downhill. Hold his downhill hand and pull gently while pressing the back of your hand against his hip to force edging. During the side step explain and demonstrate how the edge is positioned to keep the ski from sliding.

Throughout your lessons, your demonstrations provide the student with visual images to imitate. You may find a slight exaggeration is necessary. When working with your student, work from the stronger side and use the touch system.

Falling and Getting Up

Explain and demonstrate the proper way to safely fall and get up. Keep the hands clear when falling.

If assistance is needed, place the student's skis across the fall line, stronger side downhill, and help the student to rock sidewise, on a count of three, to a standing position.

With some students it may be necessary to unfasten the ski bra during this maneuver. If unassisted, the student uses his strong side uphill and pushes off with the strong arm, keeping body weight forward from the waist.

Straight Run

In the beginning it is important to work toward straight running because it will reinforce better weight distribution and more symmetrical body posture. You may assist your student in this maneuver by holding the ski tips while you maintain an inverted wedge or use the two point hold.

While giving one command at a time, encourage the student to distribute weight evenly, look ahead and flex the ankles and knees forward. Repeat the straight run until the student maintains good balance and body position and becomes familiar with the equipment.

Loading Chair Lift

Introduce the chair lift by watching and explaining how others load the lift. When the student understands, move into the line and prepare to load. You may need to guide your student by holding the arm above the elbow on the stronger side and asking the attendant to slow the chair. You can use the two point hold position to move a severely involved student to the chair lift: one hand on the waist and the other on the opposite knee, moving with the student to control movement.

Move to the loading position and when the chair is about to make contact, give a clear command to sit. It may be necessary to apply pressure to the stomach to encourage

the student to bend. While riding, have the student sit back in the chair. If the student is prone to seizure, use a pole placed across the lap and insert it under the arm of the chair as a safety device. Also take this opportunity to explain how to unload.

Unloading Chair Lift

As the unloading area approaches, remove the pole and check to see if all equipment is free from the chair.

When the ski makes contact with the snow, have the student begin to rise up and move forward. You may wish to assist by using the two point hold position. Once off, clear the unloading area as quickly as possible.

Wedge Turns and Weight Transfers

An athetoid skier turns by stabilizing the hands as shown and dropping the shoulder, pointing elbow toward heel and steering the feet.

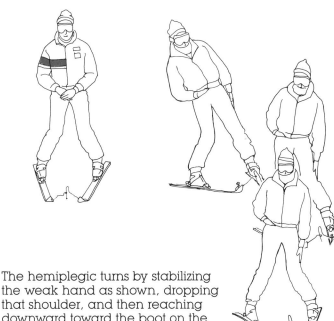

The hemiplegic turns by stabilizing the weak hand as shown, dropping that shoulder, and then reaching downward toward the boot on the strong side and steering the feet.

Wedge Turns

For individuals who can form a wedge without increasing spasticity, begin with a tip assist. While moving, repeat over and over the turning instructions:

— Drop your elbow down to the heel of your boot;
— Come to center;
— Slide your hand to the heel of the boot;
— Come to center.

Then have the student try unassisted.

Wide Track Parallel Turns

Although some students are capable of performing the wedge, for many it will increase spasticity, so teaching wide track parallel turns is recommended. Utilize gentle terrain to introduce beginning parallel turns. Use the two point hold position for either wedge or wide track parallel.

Have the student steer both feet and knees into the hill to perform an uphill christie. The uphill christie turn should be repeated in both directions until the student is capable of turning to a stop unassisted. If the student indicates that he has sufficient lateral control, try removing the stabilizers from the tips of the skis. After your student can successfully do an uphill christie in both directions, introduce linked wide track parallel turns. Explain and demonstrate a series of turns. Point out how to ski slightly in and out of the fall line, how to utilize the christie to link your turns, how to equalize the arc of each turn in both directions, and how to develop a rhythm so that the turns are fluid.

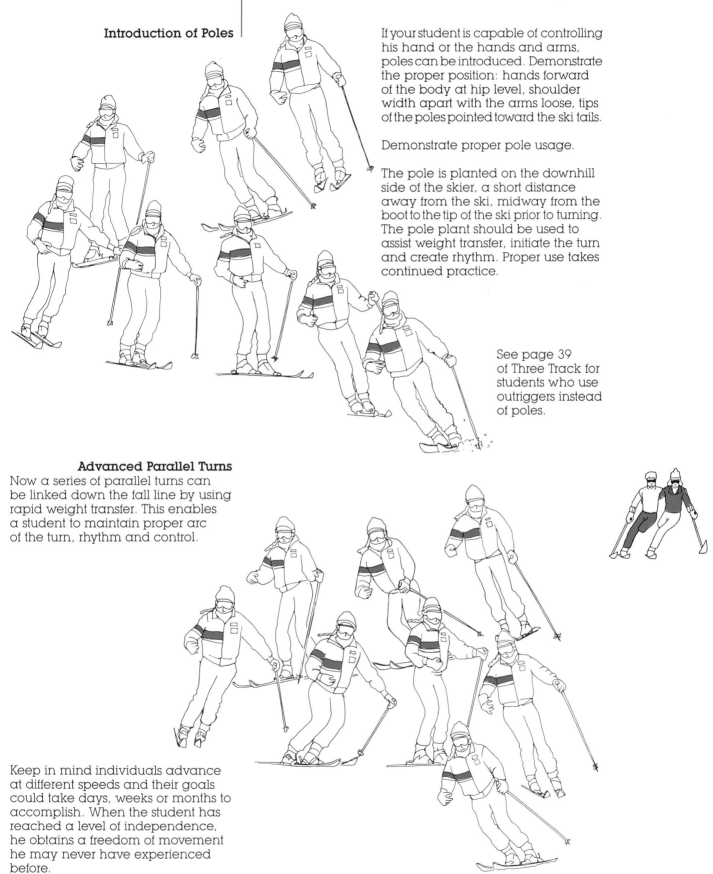

Introduction of Poles

If your student is capable of controlling his hand or the hands and arms, poles can be introduced. Demonstrate the proper position: hands forward of the body at hip level, shoulder width apart with the arms loose, tips of the poles pointed toward the ski tails.

Demonstrate proper pole usage.

The pole is planted on the downhill side of the skier, a short distance away from the ski, midway from the boot to the tip of the ski prior to turning. The pole plant should be used to assist weight transfer, initiate the turn and create rhythm. Proper use takes continued practice.

See page 39 of Three Track for students who use outriggers instead of poles.

Advanced Parallel Turns

Now a series of parallel turns can be linked down the fall line by using rapid weight transfer. This enables a student to maintain proper arc of the turn, rhythm and control.

Keep in mind individuals advance at different speeds and their goals could take days, weeks or months to accomplish. When the student has reached a level of independence, he obtains a freedom of movement he may never have experienced before.

Perhaps nowhere is ATS more readily the basis of instruction than in teaching the blind. The basic adaptation is in communicating through talk and touch to replace the function of vision. This section provides hands-on teaching tips. Essentially, all blind skiers can learn ATS and are two track skiers.

Blind people are capable of being taught to ski in a very short period of time and can become very proficient and capable of skiing moderate to difficult terrain, including moguls.

Adaptive Equipment The degree of visual impairment can vary from legal blindness to total blindness.

First Steps Speak to the visually impaired student to make her aware of your presence. Modulate your voice, speaking clearly and looking directly at the individual. Do not raise your voice if she does not have a hearing impairment. You want to instill confidence, making sure you are communicating.

Note that the blind skier can use a ski bra to establish early balance.

Be aware of the skier's balance and any problems she might be having with inner ear equilibrium — the source of her balance. Do not take her arm, but permit her to take yours. Be aware of barrier problems: stairs, curbs, change in terrain, snow and ice, and other obstacles. Give only one command at a time, making it short and concise.

When walking in a crowded area, have the student place her hand on your shoulder and walk behind you. Walk at the student's pace. Keep the student informed as to her location and where she is heading. Paint a picture with words. The blind understand through description.

Introduction of Ski Equipment The introduction of ski equipment should take place indoors, prior to the actual lesson.

The totally blind person relies on feel. Therefore, when introducing equipment, the blind person should be permitted to know exactly what the equipment feels like and what it does.

Let the student handle the boot. Assist her in putting on the boot, explaining proper fit and why support is necessary. She should be permitted to put on the other boot by herself.

"This check comes from a totally blind young man who has benefitted greatly from his experiences at Winter Park. He wanted to help others, as he himself has been helped."

In the beginning, blind people find it difficult to walk in ski boots, as they are heavy and clumsy. Make sure the student takes your arm securely to maintain balance.

Permit the student to explore the ski, beginning with the tip, moving downward to the toe piece of the binding and explain how the toe of the boot is inserted into the toe piece. Move to the heel piece, explaining the mechanism and how it locks the heel of the boot in place. From there move toward the tail of the ski.

If she has no questions, turn the ski over and, starting with the tip, make her aware of the sharp metal edges and caution her to be careful as she runs her hand along the edge of the ski. Explain the reason for the groove and edges.

Explain the ski pole, allowing the student to feel the grip, shaft, basket and point of the pole. Explain why the pole should not be carried in such a manner that the point might injure anyone nearby, nor should it be placed ahead of the skier while moving. Make her aware that the pole is used to assist in walking and for balance and eventually in the skiing technique.

Give the student time to gain a mental picture of the equipment. Once she has had sufficient time to inspect and understand the equipment, she is ready, with the aid of an instructor, to put on the skis.

Putting on Skis

The skis should be cold before placing them on the snow. After the instructor has assisted the student in putting on one ski, the student is allowed to put on the other ski. If poles with straps are being used, the student should not put her hands through the straps, as they can catch on something.

Walking on the Flat

It is possible that the student has never been in the position to feel a sliding motion while maintaining balance. In the beginning she needs to work with this new feeling so that she can obtain a sense of balance and feeling for the texture of the snow.

Walk her in a straight line, guiding her by putting your hand on top of her pole or by skiing in front, tapping the poles for sound.

It is important at this point to allow the student to be totally independent, since independence is the first step towards secure balance.

Walking in a Circle Directed by Clicking of Instructor's Poles

After the student has successfully walked in a straight line, the instructor should guide her in the direction of a large circle, permitting the student to become more familiar with the equipment. She should slowly adjust to the weight of the skis, the approximate length of the skis and the feel of maneuvering them and maintaining balance.

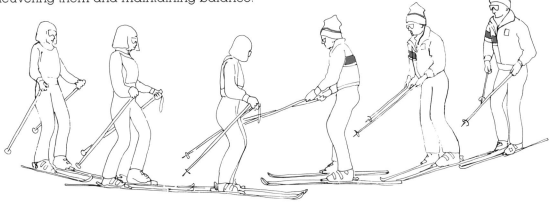

The instructor should look for the spreading of the tips of the skis, as this is quite common to the beginner. Instruct the student to keep her feet parallel to one another.

When speaking to a beginner, always refer to the feet rather than to the skis, as it is difficult for her to relate to the skis. In commanding the student to bring her feet parallel to one another, ask her to bring her toes in. She will readily understand this command.

Body Position: Touch System

From the beginning, the student should be taught in such a manner that she is able to understand the technique and each maneuver prior to moving on to a new one. Frustration can destroy the desire to succeed if the instructions are not clear.

Use the touch system. If the student is not aware of the required flex in the ankles and knees, touch her when the commands are given. Since she has no visual assistance, technique cannot be demonstrated. To prevent frustration, good communication through touch must be established.

On flat terrain, the instructor should explain hand position, which should be forward, just below the hips. Touch the student's ankles, knees and waist, explaining the proper flex in these areas. Explain again to the student how important it is for her to keep her weight forward.

Problems frequently occurring are incorrect position of hands, lack of flex in ankles and knees, and weight resting back on heels.

Proper body position is difficult for a blind student to comprehend. Therefore, it is important that the instructor literally mold her into position by means of touch and verbal command. The fall line should always be used for the teaching of straight running. This can enhance balance tremendously.

Side Stepping

Once the student has become comfortable with her skis while walking in a straight line and in circles, she is ready to climb the beginner hill.

Stand opposite the student, instructing her to place the skis across the hill. Utilizing side stepping techniques, instruct the student to roll her knees into the hill in order to edge the skis while taking short steps, making sure the ski poles do not get in the way. At first, don't take the student more than 15 to 20 feet up the hill.

Exercise: If student has a problem, simulate climbing on stairs.

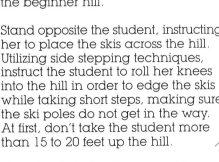

Finding the Fall Line

Once the student has reached this distance, inform her as to where the fall line is located. Have the student place her ski pole just forward of the tips of her skis and move the pole in a half circle from side to side, to determine where the fall line is.

Straight Run

Once she is aware of the location of the fall line, instruct her to place the poles downhill in preparation for turning her skis into it. Care should be taken that the poles are at least shoulder width apart, permitting the student to bring the skis around into the fall line. The skis should be moved with short steps. If the student has difficulty, the instructor may assist by holding the tips of the skis until the student is in position.

The student should be permitted to move down the hill in a straight run. This maneuver should be repeated several times.

Falling and Getting Up

Practice, with assistance, a fall and then how to get up so the student learns the sensation and correct method.

Getting Up Unassisted

Have the student try this method or alternate method 2 shown on page 80 of Developmentally Disabled.

Gliding Wedge

On flat terrain, instruct the student to lift the heels of the boots outward, forming a wedge. After she understands that the wedge position is maintained by keeping the tails of the skis outward by pressure from inside the heel of the boot, she should be permitted to attempt the maneuver.

Once the student is in position on the hill, have her repeat the maneuver as she was instructed. Make sure she understands that the hips should be centered between the skis, hands should be held forward and slightly below the waist, knees and ankles flexed forward. Encourage her to move down the fall line in a relaxed position.

Use touch system to assist in wedge position.

The student follows the clicking sound of instructor's poles.

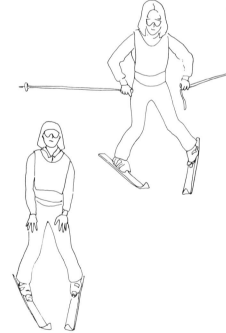

This illustration shows a typical incorrect body position, easily remedied by removing poles and having the student place hands on thighs.

A bamboo pole is an aid in teaching a wedge. Illustration 2 demonstrates a stop. Instruct the student to remain forward on the balls of the feet when stopping.

To Stop

Once she has become secure with the gliding wedge, introduce a controlled wedge to a stop. At this time the instructor can decide whether the student is ready for the chair lift.

**Chair Lift
Loading** | Describe the chair lift and explain loading and unloading procedures.

Always use the patrol or employee entrance.

Explain to the student how to hold her poles and have her take your arm as you lead her to the loading area. The blind student should load on the inside, closest to the lift attendant. Explain the chair as it approaches. Instruct your student to sit when the chair touches the back of her legs.

Unloading When preparing to unload, keep tips up, place feet down on the snow, have the blind student take your arm, stand up and remain forward (do not wedge). Guide the student out of the unloading area.

Controlled Wedge

A controlled wedge is properly executed by moving the tails of the skis slightly wider than the gliding wedge, permitting the student to create a resistance against the snow, by utilizing the inside edges to slow speed.

Frequently problems occur when the student does not understand body position. If problems occur, reinforce by tapping the inside of the boot. Hip projection from one side to the other can cause one side to be flat and the other to be rolled on edge. The instructor can correct this by skiing behind the student, placing his hands on the student's hips and centering her weight over the skis. The student should practice this maneuver for some time in order to perfect control, body position and balance.

Linking Wedge Turns

Instruct the student to initiate a turn by steering both feet in the direction of travel while maintaining a wedge. Permit the student to link her turns in and out of the fall line. Make sure timing and rhythm are used in order to make a smooth transition from one direction to another.

Do not use "Right" or "Left." Permit the student to choose the direction. Once she has chosen the direction, use the commands "Turn" or "Go."

The blind student has difficulty in equalizing the arc of the turn in either direction. The instructor should correct this with verbal commands, instructing the student to complete each turn. The uphill christie to a stop can help in understanding proper arc of a turn.

It is very important for a blind student to use a steered turn. She should be made aware of the fact that the turns are initiated by turning both feet and knees at the same time in the direction of travel. If she does not utilize both feet at the same time, crossing of the skis will occur.

The instructor becomes a magnet for the student through verbal commands and the clicking of poles. Move the student through turns.

Uphill Christie

From the parallel position (never in a wedge) use the connecting arm to guide the student out of the fall line into the christie, enabling her to feel the proper initiation and arc of a turn.

Beginning Parallel Turns

Beginning parallel turns utilize the same technique as in controlled wedge turns. To begin parallel turns, encourage the student to release outward pressure on both skis just after the initiation of the turn, permitting the skis to assume the wide track parallel position. Use moderate teaching terrain for this maneuver.

Pole Planting

After the student has successfully acquired the wide track parallel position and can turn in both directions, introduce pole planting. The right pole is planted to go to the right, the left pole is planted to go to the left. Introduce pole planting by tapping the pole of the student and talking through the motion of planting the pole. This should be done on both sides so that the student understands the technique.

The pole should be planted just forward of the feet and to the side. The pole is planted at the beginning of the turn, taking care that the student completes the turn prior to preparing for the next pole plant. Often the student will neglect to complete the arc of the turn and will initiate a pole plant in the next direction too soon, destroying rhythm and motion.

This maneuver can be very difficult to grasp and has to be practiced to get the right timing.

Advanced Parallel Turns Utilizing the wide track parallel position, encourage the student to increase the arc of the turn, displacing both tails

in order to control speed. This will create a slight rebound, permitting the student to advance into the next turn without hesitation.

Emphasize control, timing and rhythm. Familiarize the student with skiing under control by utilizing carved turns, with emphasis on the completion of turns and the displacement of both tails.

As the student becomes more proficient and is skiing faster, ski as close as possible to the student. Communication is of the utmost importance at this advanced stage.

In teaching the deaf to ski, there are a few basic things to learn about deafness. The principal problem of the deaf is communication. Since they cannot hear, it is difficult for them to learn to talk. The problem is not the same for all hearing impaired; there are varying degrees of deafness. For some, hearing aids are a great help; for others, no help at all; for a few, a great annoyance. Cold weather can make a hearing aid misbehave, causing the student to lose his partial hearing. The hearing aid itself may loosen in the cold and be difficult to keep in position.

Some hearing impaired students can "read lips." The amount of the English language that appears on the lips is only approximately 30 percent. The other 70 percent is picked up from context plus a lot of guessing. Some deaf have a knack for reading lips and others never master it. Lip reading is more of an art than a science.

"It was nice to see instructors be able to sign."

All the deaf carefully watch your face and your body language in order to understand what you are trying to communicate. Make sure your student can see your face clearly. Don't turn your head, don't cover your lips, be sure your face is not in shadow, keep eye contact. A full beard, a cigarette, cigar or pipe in your mouth while talking, mumbling, not moving your lips and moving your lips too much will all defeat those who can lip read.

Most of the totally deaf depend on sign language (American Sign Language — ASL) for communication. ASL is basically a foreign language. Take the time to learn at least the basic signs needed to teach your student to ski safely. If you go beyond this with your sign language, you will be able to chat and share ideas with your student. Wearing ski gloves rather than mittens makes signing easier. The Hotfingers cross country gloves work well and keep hands reasonably warm.

You may come across a pupil, totally deaf, who is strictly "aural." He speaks and reads lips with varying ability but does not know sign language. You may or may not understand his speech. Some speak very well but some are unintelligible. With them, communicating can be very difficult.

Although communication is the principal problem in teaching the deaf to ski, one other problem that may surface is an inner ear problem which makes balance difficult. With some students, skiing has helped overcome the problem.

Teach the deaf student to ski by example and imitation. Indicate what you want your student to do, show him, have him do it, make necessary corrections. Always ski in front of him, backwards if necessary, so he can see what you are doing, your signing and your expression. Show or tell him what he is doing right. Instruct, but don't get too technical. Emphasize the fun of skiing, but also teach control so that he can ski safely.

The techniques for the deaf are basically the same as for the hearing, adapted from ATS.

Manual Alphabet

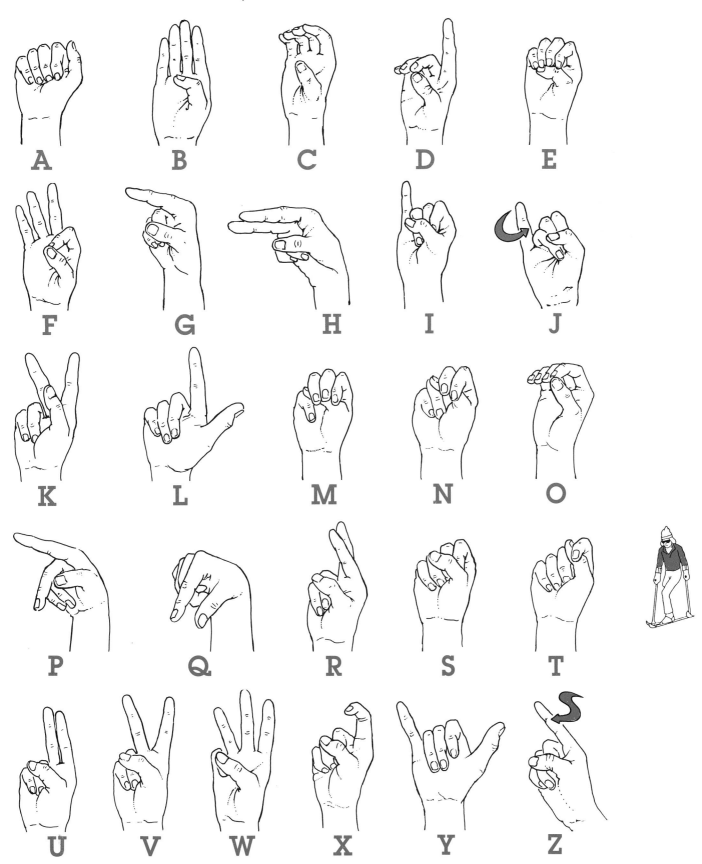

Sign Language
for Skiing

arms	bathroom	boots	boss	careful
careless	control	do	don't, not	
equal	excellent	fall down	fast, quick	
fingerspell	flex	flex knees	flex ankles	

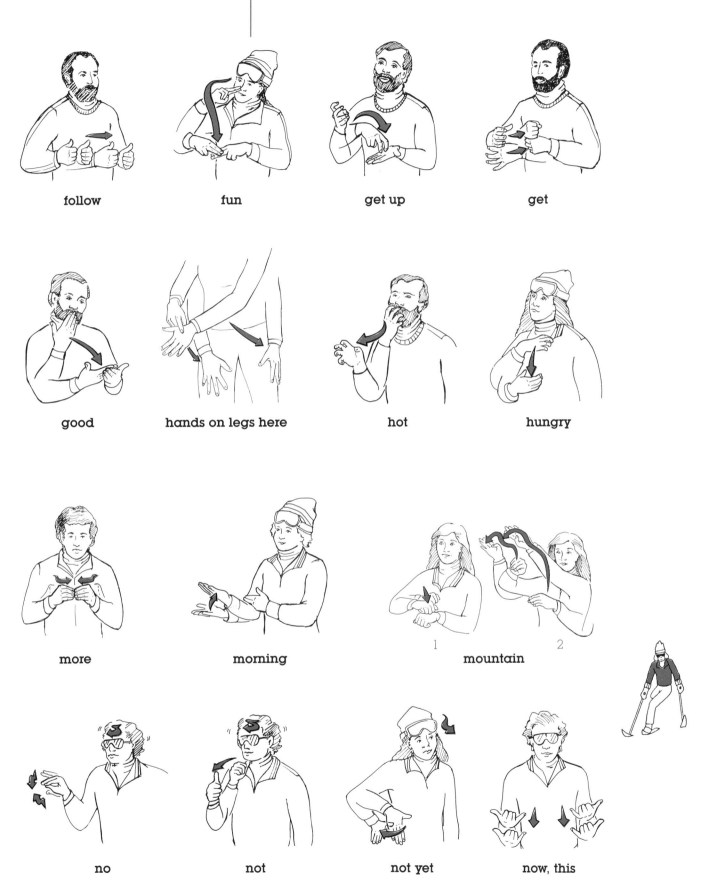

follow

fun

get up

get

good

hands on legs here

hot

hungry

more

morning

mountain

no

not

not yet

now, this

pay attention

ride

right, correct

rotary, turn

safety

same

ski

ski pole

slow

snow

stand

1

2

3

4

sun safety

that, stay

thirsty

those

tree

wait

walk

warm

watch

weight

what

wind

winter, cold

wonderful

yes

you

Managing the Student

In working with the developmentally disabled, you are basically using the American Teaching System. However, you aren't modifying technique as much as you are their behavior and your communication with them. The key is to make it fun and create a positive atmosphere.

Adaptive Equipment

Use a ski bra if the student is unable to form a wedge — but only as a training device, so that the student doesn't become dependent on it.

Beginning Instruction

Beginning instruction is taught on a one-to-one basis for two reasons: the student can identify with one individual; safety can be maintained at all times.

When the instructor is introduced to the student, the instructor should have already been informed as to any type of medication, medical problems or any behavioral idiosyncrasies.

Frequently behavioral problems can arise and cause great frustration for both the student and the instructor. Some of the behavioral problems can be prevented if the instructor makes it perfectly clear from the very beginning who is in charge. This will give the student a definite feeling of direction and alleviate possible manipulation.

To prevent confusion, it is necessary to be explicit in your instruction. For example, when a beginning student is instructed to side step up a teaching hill, a ski pole can be utilized to designate the distance he is required to climb. Objects such as a ski pole serve as visual aids in measuring distances and can prevent the frustration that may be caused by not being properly informed as to the task at hand.

The instructor should learn to modulate his voice and treat the developmentally disabled individual according to his chronological age.

The student should be permitted to interact socially. Experiences such as skiing can assist psychologically in growth and development.

Body Position

The touch system is the only way to communicate proper body position to a developmentally disabled student: hands on thighs; flex in ankles, knees and hips; raise chin to look ahead.

"It was beautiful to watch the students improve and talk about their success. It opened some doors to inner happiness and pride — a gift that will last forever."

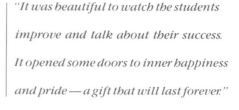

Do not allow the student to grasp or hang on to you. Be firm in your discipline.

Walking

Walking the student on the flat will disclose perceptual problems.

Side Stepping See page 65 of Visually Impaired for further explanation.

Use the downhill arm as a rudder to keep the student across the fall line while side stepping.

Straight Run Reinforce body position for straight run, using assist.

Hands on thighs in unassisted straight run.

To Fall Teach the student to fall on her uphill hip.

To Get Up With skis across fall line and hands uphill just forward of the feet, walk hands down the hill and push upward to a standing position.

An alternative way of getting up is to have the student lie up the fall line, position feet in an inverted wedge, pushing up off the snow, chest first, then hips.

Wedge To prevent student from sliding backward, assist her out of the fall line. This maneuver could also be utilized to assist student into fall line to begin a turn.

The instructor signals a wider wedge and taps the pressure points.

Further frustrations can be prevented if the instructor works from in front of the student. The instructor will be in a better position visually to demonstrate various ski positions and techniques. In addition to learning from the visual demonstrations, the student gains a sense of security with the instructor ahead of him and nearby. This also enhances safety.

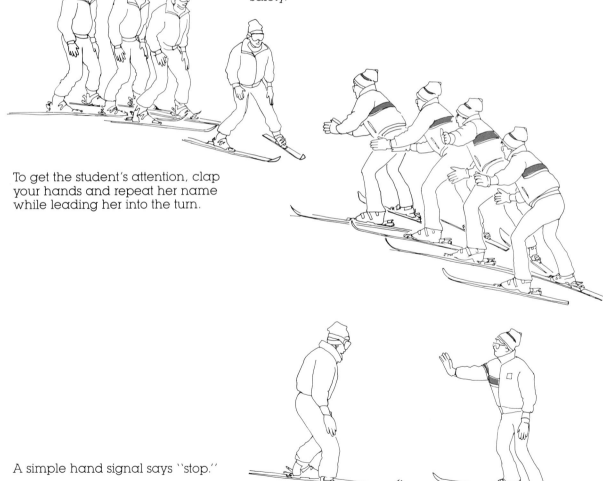

To get the student's attention, clap your hands and repeat her name while leading her into the turn.

A simple hand signal says "stop."

Sit skiing permits severely disabled individuals previously unable to ski to experience the thrill of speed and motion. Sit skiing was introduced in the 1980 Winter Park teaching program and became an immediate success. Over 440 lessons were provided the first season on a trial basis to paraplegics, incomplete quadriplegics and many other persons. The sit ski is a sled-like device that is controlled by the upper body and short, hand-held poles. Safety of the sit skier and other skiers is ensured at all times by "tethering," in which an able-bodied skier skis behind the sled holding an attached rope.

Sit skiing can be a tremendous joy for those dependent on a wheelchair. While on the ski slopes these individuals experience a fluidity of motion in a barrier-free environment once thought unobtainable.

"Your sled program is the most exciting thing I've done in the 10½ years of being a quad."

Evaluation
When first introduced to your student, you and a qualified staff person will evaluate his special needs. Is he a para- or low-injury quad? Does he require a wheelchair for mobility? What is his overall health and physical condition?

Adaptive Equipment
During the evaluation you have found out how well the student can grasp. This will determine what kind of poles the student will use. The most common are the spike and kayak types. While in the equipment room, take the opportunity to explain some of the sit ski's features to the student, such as the roll bar, main shell and edges.

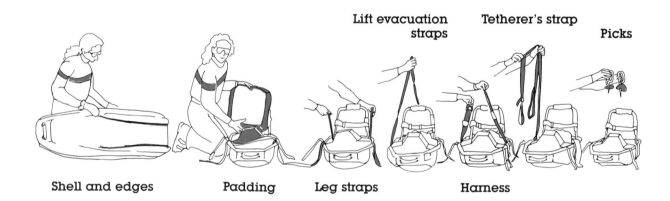

Shell and edges   Padding   Leg straps   Lift evacuation straps   Harness   Tetherer's strap   Picks

Clothing
While in the sit ski, snow has a tendency to fly up into the face of the skier so proper clothing is an important factor. Goggles, a hat and a waterproof jacket should be worn.

Special care should be taken with quads and paras. Since they have little or no feeling in their lower body, frostbite can easily set in. Use insulated boots to protect the feet from frostbite. Layered clothing should also be worn so the body temperature can be adjusted depending on the amount of physical activity. Waterproof mittens or gloves are a must.

Getting Into Sit Ski The student should be made comfortable in the sit ski. It is very important that the knees be slightly bent and the knee pad placed under the knees. This is to prevent hyperextension.

Check that the two front yellow straps are laid up alongside of the sit ski for easy access in case of a chair evacuation. Finally, check for any loose lines hanging out of the sled. At this point the student is now ready for the chair lift.

Lift from wheelchair into sit ski

Attaching straps

Snow skirt over the head

Loading Chair Lift To help ease the student's apprehension, explain how the sit ski has been designed to be compatible with the chair. Have the lift operator slow the chair. Then have the student push himself up to the chair if at all possible. While loading, grasp the roll bar on the side with one hand and with the other hand grasp the front side of the sit ski. When the sit ski is in position, fasten the safety strap and instruct the student not to lean forward.

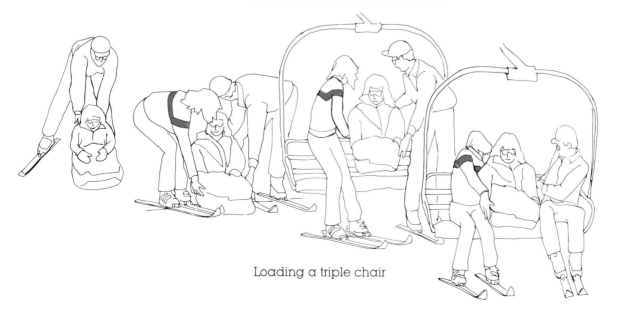

Loading a triple chair

Loading a double chair

Looking for approaching chair   Positioning sit ski   Attaching safety strap

Unloading Chair Lift When approaching the unloading area, signal the chair lift operator to slow the lift. Release the safety strap. Utilizing the same hand position as when loading, tilt forward and push off as soon as the front of the sit ski makes contact with the snow. Guide the sit ski with the roll bar away from the unloading area.

Emergency Lift Evacuation If there is a chair lift breakdown, it will be necessary to evacuate the sit ski. For this reason the chair lift harness should be easily accessible while riding the lift. Lower the snow skirt and remove the two front yellow straps. Pull out the third strap from behind the student. Attach them to the carabiner. The assembly is then attached to the safety patrol rope. Release the safety strap. As the patrol begins to lift the sit ski out, guide it sideways away from the chair until it clears and is lowered.

85 | TEACHING: Sit Ski

How to Fall and to Roll For a sit skier, a fall means the rolling of the sit ski. The roll should be practiced on gentle terrain at first. Instruct your student never to try to stop a roll. It is very easy for an arm to get caught underneath. This maneuver should not be taught to students who have recently had a back fusion.

Tetherer Explain to your student the purpose of the tetherer, how it serves as a safety mechanism in case the sit ski gets out of control. Explain the fall line. Also explain how the uphill or inside edges are used to carve a turn.

Tethered Stop Because the sit ski's response is greatly altered in different snow conditions, pay close attention to the condition of the hill. The sit ski works best in soft packed snow or just after a snow fall. Extra caution should be taken on hard packed snow or icy conditions. From the beginning the student should be aware that the sit ski will not turn as sharply or stop as fast as a pair of skis. This needs to be stressed, especially to those students that have skied normally before their injury. Emphasize to the student that caution should be taken when skiing through a congested area.

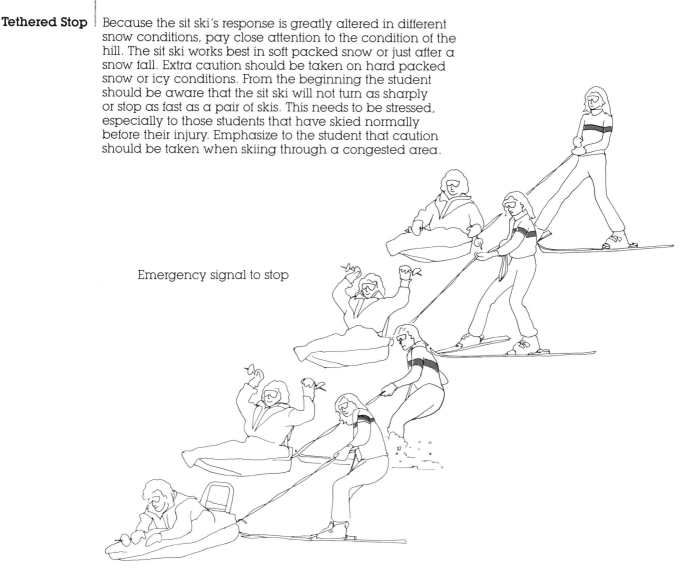

Emergency signal to stop

Straight Run On moderate terrain, introduce the straight run. This will help the student ``feel'' the equipment and find balance while moving.

To Stop When turning to a stop, have the student ski down the fall line. The pole is then planted on the uphill side as the student leans into the hill. Practice this maneuver in both directions. If the student has difficulty in stopping, the tetherer will bring the sit ski under control by utilizing a hockey stop position.

Pole Plant It is the pole plant that initiates the turn. Work on rhythm and upper body weight shift with your student to help understand how to work the sit ski's edges in carving a turn.

Beginning Turns When teaching beginning turns, stress the need for smooth arc turns. Have the student start setting the next turn just before the sit ski enters the fall line.

Linked Advanced Turns When working with the linked turns, it is important for the tetherer to develop anticipation skills. Anticipate when the student will turn and turn with him. Otherwise, you may get whiplashed to another position and be unable to help the student.

Work toward tighter turns on intermediate terrain. At some point suggest to your student the idea of having one of his friends become a certified tetherer. This will give the sit skier and his friend the freedom to ski at their leisure.

Since team work is very important in the moguls, explain the difficulty a tetherer has when following the sit skier. For instance, the sit skier should go around moguls, not over them. Excessive speed in rough terrain can also cause problems for the tetherer in case an emergency stop is required.

Sit skiing has given the individual who normally utilizes a wheelchair the opportunity to become an active participant in the sport of skiing, but safety must be stressed at all times.

The mono-ski is now replacing the Arroya sit ski as the equipment of the future for most paraplegics. The mono-ski allows this disability actually to ski in a three track fashion. Designed in West Germany about six years ago, the mono-ski was only made available in the United States in the fall of 1985. Previously it was used only in a few European countries and designed strictly for the T-bar, not chair lifts. To enable the West Germans to market the mono-ski in the United States, certain modifications were made to their mono-ski.

At this time, there are two versions of the mono-ski in this country. The GFL is the modified West German model. It has a shell in which the mono-skier sits and a loading mechanism that depends on a pin that must be released when loading the chair, then re-inserted before skiing. Because of the slight complexity of the mechanism, the GFL requires two people to operate: the skier and an instructor or assistant who knows how to handle the pin.

A new design for the mono-ski is now in production. Its main feature is a self-loading mechanism that eliminates the problems of the pin and simplifies the loading of the chair lift, allowing the mono-skier to ski more independently. It has a chassis instead of a shell. This new design reacts quickly, like a competitive ski, but can be used in the same teaching sequence with a beginning mono-skier who feels comfortable with it. The illustrations in this section show the newer design, with a prototype shell. More information on both models is in the Resources section.

Evaluation

If the individual is athletic and in excellent shape, it is possible for an injury level as high as T-4 to use the mono-ski. However, a higher level of injury may lack necessary balance and strength. See the Disabilities Definitions on Spinal Cord Injuries.

Most beginning mono-skiers probably began skiing in the sit ski. It is an advantage to have experience with reading terrain, building up endurance in the arms, back and abdomen, and getting experience with chair lift procedures. If the student has never been skiing before his injury, skiing in the sit ski might be a good idea.

A method of evaluating a student's strength and balance capabilities is to have him sit in the mono-ski and attempt to push the ski to an upright position from a 45° angle.

Adaptive Equipment

With injury levels above T-10, a higher seat belt may be desirable, not only for support but to give the skier more ability to lean forward and sideways and transfer weight for the initiation of the turn. The skier should fit as snugly as possible into the seat to provide a response to the ski just as a ski boot serves a stand-up skier. Short adjustable outriggers are used by the mono-skier.

Getting into Ski

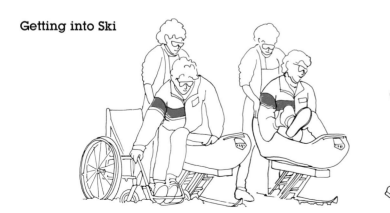

Help the student transfer from his wheelchair while stabilizing the mono-ski.

Body Position and Balance

Define center of balance concept, based on trunk position and arm placement.

Balance Drills: (1) Practice with outriggers how to stay up, relaxing arms and keeping elbows unlocked; (2) Bend upper body forward and back; (3) Twist upper body right and left; (4) Swing arms forward and back together and in opposition.

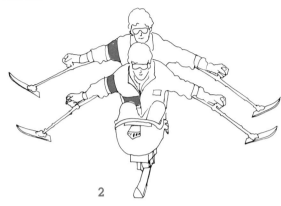

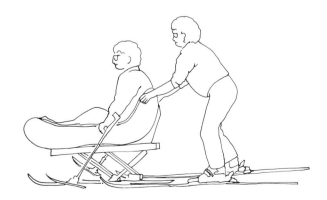

Starting Out

Choose flat terrain — a loosely packed, groomed slope for slow speed.

Moving on the Flat

The instructor, with or without skis, holds firmly onto the rear of the shell and pushes the student along.

To Fall   Have the student practice placement of outriggers. Outriggers should be in the snow and forward, elbows tucked in and locked. In falling over, tell him not to attempt to break the fall. (A variety of injuries may result.)

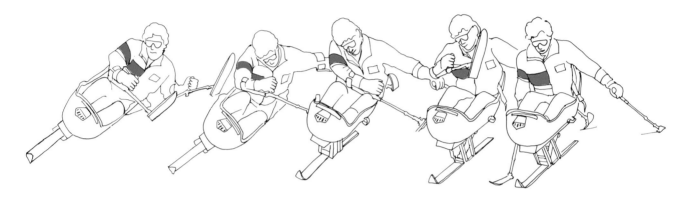

To Get Up   To get up unassisted, have the student position the mono-ski across the fall line, with body uphill. Place outriggers uphill and push up with edge of tail of outrigger ski and rebalance. If necessary, the instructor can assist from behind.

Skiing on Flat Terrain With Able-Bodied Support   The instructor, without skis, holds on to the back of the student's shell and pushes the student up a slight incline and then gives support going down the hill. Begin discussing outrigger placement for skiing. The outriggers should be placed on the snow, close to the sides of the mono-ski shell, positioned forward at approximately a 60° angle.

The instructor, with skis, holding firmly onto the rear of the shell, assists the skier with gentle turns downhill. Discuss the concept of a basic turn. Complete each turn to a stop. The student should feel some control and ability to stop. Now you are ready for the chair lift.

Loading the Chair Lift

A) The instructor assists in getting the mono-ski into position. The student pulls the lever which elevates the mono-ski, making it compatible with the chair lift for loading.

B) The chair lift attendant helps stabilize the mono-ski and prevents the chair lift from swinging while loading.

C) The skier and instructor sit in the chair. Note that his right outrigger is behind her to prevent slipping.

D) The instructor fastens the safety line to the back of the chair with carabiner.

In the GFL model the pin must be released from the shell to allow the ski to separate from the shell. To do this, the skier pushes up on his outriggers to unweight the shell. The instructor pulls the pin out to release the shell, then immediately pushes the pin back into place once the shell has cleared the pin.

Move into position until the back of the mono-ski aligns with the "Stand Here" line. Ask the lift attendant to stabilize the chair. As the chairlift approaches, lift the seat portion of the mono-ski only, so that the mono-ski will slide onto the chair.

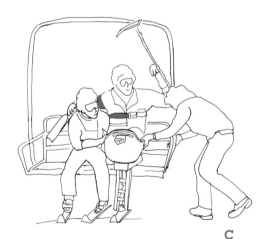

Once the mono-ski is loaded on the chair the instructor should pull back on the shell to be sure it is squarely on the chair lift and also attach a safety line with a carabiner to the back of the chair. The instructor can also assist on some models by putting her arm in front of the mono-skier's chest and pushing back gently but firmly from this position as well.

Unloading the Chair Lift

Remove the safety strap/carabiner. Prepare to unload by sliding forward on the seat of the chair lift. Have the student put the outriggers out to each side in preparation for skiing off the ramp.

The instructor can help by giving a push from her side of the chair. This motion should be done as a "wiggle" back and forth, gently but firmly. The instructor should always have a firm grasp on the shell handles so that they will not unload too early. Make sure the shell points straight down the unload ramp and that the unload is as gentle as possible.

As the skier unloads from the chair, there will be a bounce as the shell drops onto the spring/ski. The skier should be prepared to balance himself with the outriggers and ski off the ramp. Remember to replace the pin (depending on model) to secure the shell back onto the spring/ski.

Chair Lift Evacuation

Each ski area has its own evacuation procedures. The best advice here is to stage a mock evacuation with the ski patrol at least once a season, preferably at the beginning of each season. The mono-ski and the skier should be equipped with an evacuation harness that is properly adjusted and is secured.

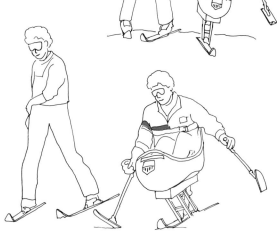

Basic Turns, Assisted

Choose gentle terrain — a loosely packed slope with a good run out. Define and practice a basic emergency stop. To stop, the student leans uphill, arms in proper position, and falls uphill. With instructor assistance, the student should practice turns with outriggers in front, traversing the slope to control speed, linking the next turn. Several runs will be necessary.

Basic Turns, Unassisted

Have the student try unassisted turns on a flat ski and making shallow, linked turns in the fall line. He uses his hips to make the weight shift, blocking his shoulders downhill, and the outriggers to initiate the turn. This is comparable to learning to steer a gliding wedge for able-bodied skiers.

Edging

Introduce the edging concept with able-bodied assistance and demonstration by the instructor.

Slip Edge Drill: Side slip to uphill edge without assistance; repeat across slope. The student should lead with the downhill outrigger and lean weight forward to initiate a turn (rocking motion), then return to his center of balance. The instructor stresses leaning uphill with edge into the slope and keeping the head centered. The student should practice until proficient.

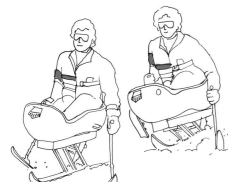

Uphill Christie or Hockey-Stop Drill: A hockey stop is a skidded stop using the uphill edge, perpendicular to the fall line, to make a quick stop. Drill should progress with increased speed; practice until proficient.

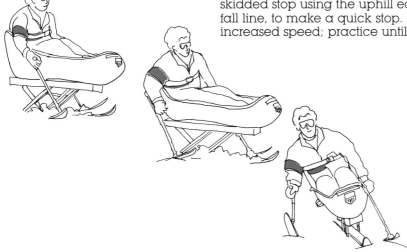

Medium Radius Turns

Begin to close the radius of the turn, no longer traversing the slope. Reduce glide time between turns.

Techniques

Body Angulation: When heading down the fall line, tell the student to keep his head centered, weighting the uphill edge with his hips and/or body weight. Use this to initiate turns. Caution him not to hold too long or skidding out will occur. To complete the turn, have him return to centered balance point and glide into fall line with unweighting motion. The motion should be similar to the angulation of able-bodied skier's ankle, knee and hip.

Balance Leaning forward helps to initiate a turn and then returning to the center of balance assists in completing turns.

Outrigger Position: Simultaneous weighting and placing the downhill outrigger forward will initiate a turn. Remind the student to unweight the downhill outrigger to complete the turn and advance the opposite outrigger to initiate the opposite turn (similar to able-bodied pole plant).

Head Position: The head must always be centered and looking down the fall line (equivalent to an able-bodied skier's shoulder/head squared placement).

Advanced Skiing

Short radius skiing involves quicker execution of narrower radius turns down the fall line. Outrigger placement should be closer in toward the shell. The lead outrigger is used more to pivot turn as in an able-bodied skier's pole plant. Teach the student to push off with uphill outrigger placed in center position in order to upweight body.

Body position at this ability level depends on a shorter rocking motion of the body. The head is always looking down the fall line and centered shoulders follow the head.

"It was my first attempt at skiing since becoming a paraplegic. I never dreamed I'd be able to enjoy the thrills associated with skiing ever again."

Speed Control Tips

1. Traverse uphill when needed;
2. Wide radius turns;
3. Quicker, faster turns;
4. Attempt to remain relaxed;
5. Drag tail of outriggers.

Copy outline credit: The Breckenridge Outdoor Education Center, et al. See Acknowledgements.

The Senior Citizen Ski Program began at Winter Park during the 1980-81 ski season with ten seniors from the Denver area. Because of the overwhelming success, the program has been increased to include up to 40 seniors with a disability.

The program was developed to provide an opportunity for seniors to learn to ski with others their own age without a financial strain. Physical limitations may also prohibit seniors from enrolling in a ski school. Seniors skiing in the program are given equipment and lessons free of charge. Seniors 62-69 have to purchase a reduced price lift ticket, but those 70 and over ski free.

All the seniors involved in the program come from community recreation programs for people 55 years of age and older. If an individual is 55-61 and has a disability, he is eligible for the program.

Volunteers and instructors working in the Senior Citizen Program should be aware of physical limitations that may exist as a result of aging.

CONSIDERATIONS

Hearing Loss
Be sure to speak clearly and with enough volume so your students can hear you.

Endurance Level
Seniors may tire easily. Be aware of your students' level of endurance and don't push them too hard.

Circulation
Seniors may have poor circulation. Be sure they are dressed properly (warm gloves, hats, etc.).

Greater Liability to Fracture
To avoid fractures of the wrist, elbow, shoulder, teach your students to sit down when they fall so they won't fall on a wrist or knee. Remember seniors may be afraid to fall.

Stiffness and Slowness of Movement
Seniors who have not been exercising may experience stiffness and slowness of movement. Slow down the pace if this condition exists.

High Altitude Sickness
Seniors may have difficulty adjusting to the altitude and symptoms of high altitude sickness may occur: dizziness, nausea, headaches and vomiting. If these symptoms occur, the student should rest and seek medical attention if necessary.

Equipment
Senior skiers will need skis, boots and poles. Encourage them to use the Handicap Program's equipment. Some students will bring outdated equipment which could be potentially unsafe.

Teaching Progression
When teaching seniors to ski always stress safety, fun and learning. Safety is always the first and number one priority.

Volunteer instructors should use the American Teaching System when teaching seniors to ski.

Chair Lift
When the students have accomplished a good controlled wedge to a stop, they are ready for the chair lift. The basic procedure for the chair lift is as follows:

1. Always use the chair lift serving beginner areas.
2. Explain the proper procedure for loading and unloading when riding the chair lift.
3. Always load the student closest to the lift attendant.
4. When working with the beginning student, have the chair lift slowed down when loading and unloading.
5. Seniors in the program will have to wait in line for the chair lift.

Terrain
Always ski the senior students on beginning terrain. When they are ready to progress, have them ski a moderate run. Never ski terrain that is too difficult for them.

Teaching Tips
1. Always teach new techniques to seniors on the flat.
2. Never side step seniors up the hill more than ten feet.
3. When side stepping up the hill, have them take off their uphill ski if they fatigue easily.
4. Teach from the feet up to the head.
5. Correct technique from the feet up to the head.
6. When teaching technique, keep the jargon simple.
7. When teaching turns, stress steering the feet and knees in the direction of the turn.
8. Seniors benefit from following their instructor when learning technique.

"I've had a very successful life but winning a first in the Seniors'

Slalom was the best ever!"

Often adaptive equipment is used only in the beginning teaching phases. The goal is to eliminate it as the student progresses.

Bucket

This prosthesis is presently in the experimental stage, to be used by an individual with a hip disarticulation. Hopefully there will soon be a better design of the hip and knee flexation available in order to permit getting onto and off of the chair lift. Hip flexation is also used in falling and getting up.

Snow pants protect the prosthesis and keep the lower torso warm.

Bungi Cord   Elastic cord.

Bungi and Pipe   Length of pipe can be adjusted to accommodate varying needs of the student, including width of wedge. A washer is inserted between ski and knotted bungi.

Bungi Only   This allows for more mobility, i.e. sliding into lift line. Length can be adjusted as required. Many students will graduate from using the bungi after the initial learning stages.

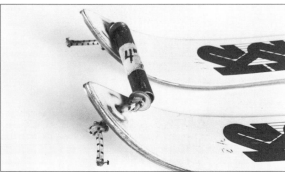 

 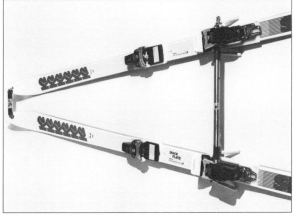

Cant

This plastic wedge, placed under the binding to equalize weight distribution, is available in various thicknesses.

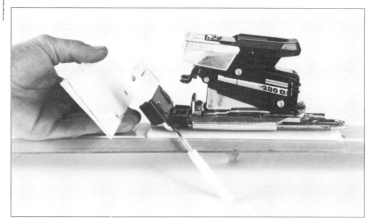

Cant in Boot Under Heel

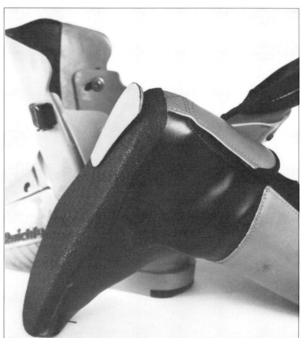

Lift

This wedge, varying in thickness, is intended to increase forward lean. A flat lateral lift should be used under the good leg to keep the hips level. A 1″ lift should be the highest used (unless working with a prosthesis); over that height requires a slant board or a plastic wedge under the binding.

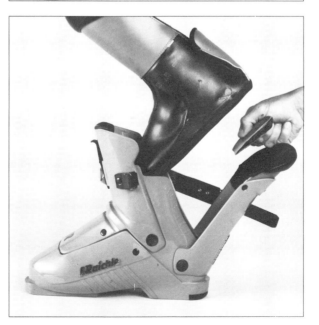

Monoboard

This is beneficial for individuals wearing full leg braces or a body brace. Bolts adjust for canting and slanting requirements.

Monoboard with Two Bindings

(approximately 8″ wide)

Mono-Ski

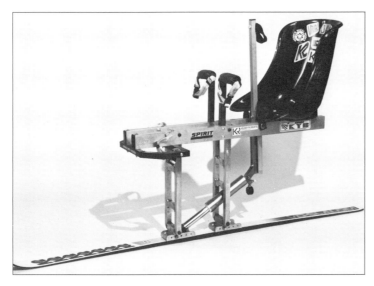

Although equipment is constantly evolving, the photo shows the most recent development. The mono-ski is shown in the "up" position for self loading onto the chair lift and "down" for the skiing position. Other models require assistance in loading the chair lift; a removable pin releases the shell from the fiberglass leaf spring, allowing the ski to drop and the shell to lift onto the chair.

Injuries above a T-7 may require a harness for more trunk support and balance.

Outrigger | Forearm crutch with 14″ ski tip mounted on a rocker base.

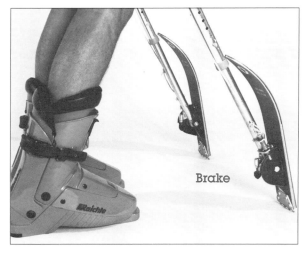

Brake

Sit Ski   Sled-type device is used by non-ambulatory individuals.

Straps, Picks, Pads and Tetherer's Strap

Snow Skirt

Neoprene material is secured around the sit skier and attached to the perimeter of the sit ski for stability and warmth.

Evacuation straps are secured by a carabiner.

A roll bar is mounted on the back of the sit ski for protection of the individual.

Ski Bra | Metal device clamped onto the tips of the skis, connected by an eyelet.

Ski Bra Trombone This device is useful for maintaining a parallel position and can slide back and forth to allow for walking and independent leg movement while skiing.

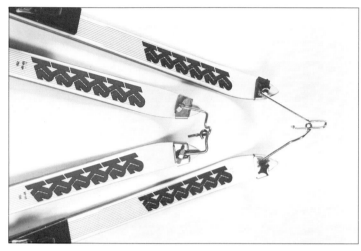

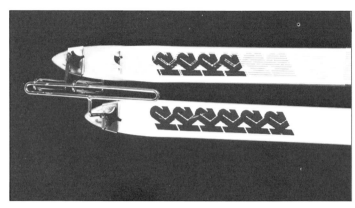

Slant Board

This board with a binding mounted on an adjustable base is used to bring an individual as close as possible to the center of gravity over the ball of the foot. It is shown here in combination with a maximum 4″ high heel lift and toe lift. Sometimes one boot will need to be positioned higher to compensate for one leg being shorter. Note that when the toes are raised, the student's outriggers must be lengthened accordingly.

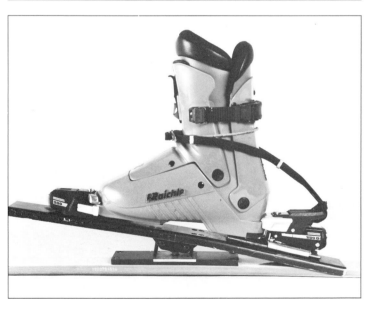

Toe Bar (or Toe Spreader)

This may or may not be used with a slant board and is usually permanently mounted to the toe piece. The turnbuckle is telescopic to adjust to various lengths.

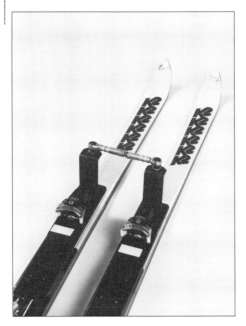

Walker with Skis and Ski Bra

Cinch

This device is used with or without a walker, mainly by children and young adults.

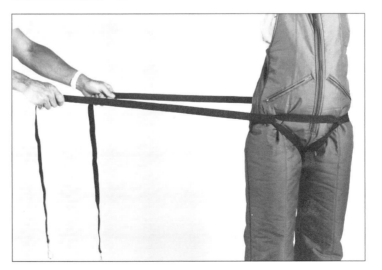

Lifeline to a Program

''Without the financial backing and support of the ski area, the Program could not exist,'' commented Hal O'Leary, Director, when talking about the first decade of the Winter Park Handicap Ski Program. For the first eight years, Winter Park supported the Program financially 100 per cent. Since then, however, the Program has generated much of its own funding through a combination of fundraising efforts and nominal charges for its services.

In order to continue the success of the Program and to meet its growing needs, fundraising efforts have had to expand. The Winter Park Recreational Association plays an extremely vital and generous role by contributing annually. Foundations and corporations with potential interest in the Program are solicited. In addition to foundation and corporate grants, there is an annual membership drive for individual donations. It is called Friends of the Handicap Program.

"I rolled all my quarters together, and here is a $150.00 donation."

Membership in Friends allows the donor to be apprised of all Handicap Program events and to receive periodic newsletters and invitations to all fundraisers. Friends also provides volunteer staff for several of the major fundraising events.

The Internal Revenue Service has designated the Winter Park Sports and Learning Center as a tax-exempt 501(C) (3) organization. Donations made to the Program are tax-deductible.

Obtaining a Foundation Grant

The grant procedures of foundations vary according to their size and staff. Most foundations have a Board of Trustees which sets overall policy and makes the ultimate decision on grants.

Initiate your contact with the foundation through the staff of the foundation, if any, to assist you in formulating the best approach to the foundation. Find and use your connections among your contacts and Board of Trustees to the Board of the foundation. Most grants are made to organizations with which there has been prior contact — some meeting or referral. Unsolicited proposals have the odds stacked against them.

Initially, the key to successful foundation solicitation is research to match your organization's needs effectively with the foundation's priorities. Your first research aim should be to identify as many as 50 top foundation prospects for your organization. Your best bet is to start with foundations that have already supported you or shown some interest in, or awareness of, your organizaation. Then go on to local foundations or foundations that you know make grants in your geographic area or to organizations like yours.

The importance of prior research can't be overstated. If your organization does not fall within the foundation's guidelines, you will not be considered for a grant. Begin your research at libraries that have been designated as Regional Centers. The following materials will help build your basic foundation library:

Foundation Center Materials — from the Foundation Center, 888 Seventh Avenue, New York, NY 10019. The Foundation Center also has more than 80 regional centers in all 50 states, generally located in local library facilities.

The Foundation Directory; The Corporate Directory — These are the standard reference books on foundations and corporations available from The Foundation Center or at a Regional Center.

The Foundation Grants Index — This annual publication gives a view of the granting interests of over 400 foundations.

Source Book Profile — Available from The Foundation Center, this looseleaf publication contains in-depth analytical profiles of the top 1,000 private and corporate foundations.

Annual Reports of Major and Local Foundations — These reports can usually be obtained through the mail from any foundation and provide background data on the foundation and its interests.

I.R.S. Forms 990 — All foundations are required to file annually with the Internal Revenue Service. The form contains basic data relating to contributions and grants paid by the foundation and names of principal officers and trustees.

Some Basic Principles of Proposal Writing

A proposal should reflect the thoughtful planning of an applicant seeking funds from a grantmaking agency in order to establish, increase or improve its services to its constituency.

Your proposal or ''case statement'' is an orderly presentation of your program and future planning to a corporation or foundation.

1. The Proposal should be Neat, Clean and Easy to Read. There should be no typographical errors in your final copy. Send an original, with copies only if the funding source requests them. Break up the copy with subheadings; nobody wants to look at a proposal that starts at the top of one page and goes on interminably, unbroken by paragraphs or some other breathing space.

   Don't use extravagant proposal packaging. Spiral bindings were made to be cut apart, and expensive covers suggest that you waste money. If you employ a very unusual format to attract attention, you risk focusing too much attention on the form of your proposal instead of its content. If you depart from the norm, do it well.

2. Write Your Proposal in Correct English.
Proposal writing is an opportunity to demonstrate your mastery of good clean English. Avoid unnecessary jargon and define your terms. To test the clarity of your writing, have friends or family read your proposal.

3. Make it Brief.
What is the proper length for a proposal? — just long enough for you to communicate your message clearly and anticipate the relevant questions. Proposals can range from two to 10 or more pages. A reasonable length is three to four pages, with enclosures.

4. Be Positive.
A positive outlook eases the proposal-writing experience. Remember that you are offering the funding source an opportunity to participate in an important, useful activity that changes lives daily. You're an applicant, not a supplicant. The funding source gets its credibility from funding winners, not losers. Often what's in it for the donor is association with a truly worthy organization doing significant work in the community.

5. Avoid Unsupported Assumptions.
The assumptions that find their way into proposals are limitless. Sometimes the applicant leads into an assumption by saying "we believe." Supporting "beliefs" with evidence and documentation is a check on logic, produces a more coherent proposal, and demonstrates your expertise to the funding source. Present enough evidence to support your position, and no more. Pages of tables, charts and graphs will probably not be read, and too often fail to support the thesis of the proposal writer. Cite sources of data in the body of the proposal and avoid footnotes.

Preparing the Case Statement: Summary

1. What's the PROBLEM?
2. WHO is affected?
3. What SOLUTIONS do you offer?
4. HOW? (actions, not methods)
5. What's the RESULT?
6. What DIFFERENCE will it make?
7. Why are you UNIQUE?
8. What will it COST?
9. What do you NEED? (be specific)
10. What's In It for the DONOR?

The Fact Sheet was developed as an informational and promotional tool. It was included in press kits and used for fundraising purposes.

Winter Park Handicap Program Fact Sheet, 1985-86

• 13,729 private ski lessons were taught to approximately 2,500 individuals in the 1985-86 season.

• 51 groups from Denver front-range schools, homes and hospitals participate in a 10-week ski program.

• 750 trained volunteers provide one-to-one instruction to approximately 1,200 students in the group programs.

Hal O'Leary

John Borelli

"It is very expensive to have a child with problems. It is hard to afford anything outside of their schooling. But your program, so inexpensive, lifted our hearts."

- The more than 45 disabilities served include blindness, amputation, multiple sclerosis, paraplegia, spina bifida, emotional disturbance, post-polio, deafness and mental retardation.

- 20 groups from the Denver area serving the more severely disabled participate in the 10-week Summer Program, with activities including whitewater raft trips, mountain climbing, nature hikes, camping trips and chair lift rides

- The largest area of growth for the Program is in the number of severely, often multiply physically and mentally disabled persons now taking up skiing due to Winter Park's ability to design adaptive equipment.

- 1,200 reduced-rate tickets were sold to handicapped "graduates" of the Program who now ski with family and friends — promoting the goal of independence while generating Program revenues

- Students come from 44 states, Australia, Canada, Europe and South America

- Primary service area is the Denver front-range region from Fort Collins to Castle Rock

- More than 75 instructor training clinics have been given for beginning ski programs in North and South America by Hal O'Leary, Director of the Ski Program

- Mr. O'Leary has received 24 awards for his outstanding service to and belief in the abilities of persons with disabilities, including the coveted "Gold Quill Award" from the National Ski Writers Association

- Last season, Winter Park started the first Handicap Ski Competition Center in the United States with 121 disabled skiers learning racing and advanced ski techniques from coaches certified to teach disabled persons

- The Sport Science Lab at Winter Park is engaged in an active evaluation and prescriptive exercise project to determine testing procedures and exercises appropriate for each disability

Lessons are given by appointment at 9:00, 11:30 and 2:00

Cost for lesson per day: $12.00*, which includes a 2-hour private lesson, lift ticket and equipment

Lift ticket per day (without lesson): $12.00*
Equipment per day (without lesson): $7.00*
Lift ticket for a "Ski Buddy," if you need assistance: $12.00

Lessons are given 7 days a week, from December 1, 1985 through April 19, 1986. Group reservations are available by special arrangement (limit: 10) by contacting the handicap office (303) 726-5514, ext. 179.

An Interview with Winter Park's Volunteer Program

In 1985-86, 850 volunteers taught 13,729 lessons to handicapped skiers. Approximately 60,000 volunteer hours are donated each year. Each volunteer instructor is required to be a strong intermediate skier and is trained to work with a specific disability.

Q. How do you get volunteers? Where do you find them?

A. By word-of-mouth — through the universities, local residents or people interested in teaching the disabled.

Q. How do you screen volunteers and how do you train them? Who trains them?

A. Volunteers are required to submit an application to the Handicap Program and must attend seven clinics: one dry-land session and six on-hill clinics. Volunteers are trained by the Handicap Program instructors who are trained by Hal O'Leary and have interned in the Handicap Program. Most of the instructors who train the volunteers are either physical therapists or have degrees in recreational therapy, special education or outdoor recreation.

Q. How often and how long is the training, covering basically what?

A. The volunteer training is held once a year from mid-November to mid-December. The clinics are held on Wednesdays, Saturdays and Sundays. Volunteers must attend six of these sessions: the first three cover training in the American Teaching Method; the final three are specialized clinics involving the specific disability with which the volunteer will be working.

Pat Kayser and Emily Quinn, accomplished sit skier.
PHOTO: JEANNE SMITH

On the Hill Clinics

Day #1 How To Teach:
1. Walking in circles — review; problems in learning
2. Side stepping
3. Straight run — proper stance on skis
4. Body position — hand position, stance on skis, flex areas
5. Gliding wedge
6. Gliding wedge with open and close — timing, rhythm
7. Gliding wedge turns — steering feet and knees in and out of the fall line

First day of clinics is most important. Demonstrations need to be slow and precise. Work on discipline and error corrections from the feet upward.

Day #2
1. Gliding wedge turn review — steering both feet and knees, body position, rhythm and timing, in and out of the fall line
2. Straight controlled wedge to stop — displacement of tails at equal angles
3. Controlled wedge turns — as with #1 but emphasizing control and fluidity in and out of fall line; steered turns
4. Wide track parallel turns — introduction

Day #3
1. Review of maneuvers to date — error correction
2. Wide track parallel turns — execution, steering, arc of turn, fall line, rhythm, timing

3. Management of students — vocabulary, commands

Day #4
1. Review of Days 1, 2 and 3 and ATS
2. Common adaptations of ATS and adaptive equipment — two point hold, skiing backward, holding ski tips, riding chair lift
3. How to handle a seizure on the chair lift and the affects of seizure control drugs
4. Disability specialization

Day #5
1. Handicap office and equipment room tour and procedures — hands-on introduction to adaptive equipment
2. Meeting times and places
3. Program coordinator assignments
4. Forms review and attendance records
5. Video viewing
6. Chair lift practice with adaptive equipment
7. Accident procedures and reports
8. Disability specialization

Day #6
1. Final review of ATS
2. Safety review
3. Falling and getting up; tour of beginning areas
4. Tour of intermediate areas for fall line maneuvers
5. Proper dress
6. Disability specialization

Q. What is the teaching schedule of the volunteer instructors?

A. They are required to teach on a weekly basis, one or two days per week, for eight to ten weeks.

Q. How many volunteer instructors do you need per number of students?

A. All instruction, with very little exception, is on a one-to-one basis.

Q. Do you compensate your volunteers in any way?

A. All volunteers are given a season pass to Winter Park for the season.

Q. Is there any feedback system from the volunteers about their students?

A. Volunteers are asked to evaluate their students each day they teach.

Q. What is the predictable turnover of volunteers?

A. Approximately 50 per cent each year.

Q. In what other ways do you use volunteers other than instructing?

A. Assisting with special events, fund raising, equipment room and some administrative assistance when needed.

"The volunteers are so well trained and very safety conscious. Capable, understanding and sensitive, their concern and interest make each kid feel special."

Notes from a Volunteer

For the first 12 winters that the Three Track Ski Club of Denver came to Winter Park, I participated as a volunteer ski instructor and chaperone with the group. At that time this was a small group of handicapped children and adults who came up to Winter Park from Children's Hospital. These first years of the program were exciting ones, for there was a pioneer spirit about them.

Each person who comes to volunteer his or her services to any group brings unique abilities and talent, along with a special wish to serve. I am an experienced ski instructor and a Physical Therapist, a good combination for this task. Consequently, it was an especially interesting and challenging experience for me — one that I cherished.

As is always the case when one steps forward to become involved, I gained more than I gave. I usually had a small group of students, some children and some adults. The first objective was safety, the second fun, the third learning to ski. Somehow the third is always realized if the first two are taking place. And we did have such fun, I more than most.

One should never make generalizations about any group. Yet there are a few characteristics of handicapped people, both children and adults, which stand out in my mind. Most particularly these courageous individuals are eager to step out and take chances. There is heightened zest and appreciation for life, a joy of accomplishment. There is a thankful spirit toward those who are helping that makes a volunteer feel very special indeed.

We met some unique challenges:

How do you teach someone to get up when he or she falls down when:

1. She has paralyzed arms and stomach muscles?
2. She has two artificial legs and two outriggers?
3. He has no legs and is skiing with a pelvic bucket and two outriggers?

How do you ride a chair lift alone in these circumstances, for the importance of independence is great?

How do you combine the need for safety with the desire for that same independence?

We had some heartbreaking times, when some of those beloved members of the group who had lost limbs to cancer finally succumbed to the disease. Yet even during the hard times, there was an uplifting emphasis on life, living and especially on loving.

Volunteering with the program has been one of the highlights of my life. I recommend it to all of you who feel the call to do so. You will be part of an area of endeavor which will surpass ordinary living and add immeasurable value to your life, and to the lives of others.

Katie Branch

WINTER PARK HANDICAP PROGRAM

VOLUNTEER APPLICATION
1987-88 SEASON

Name _____ Age _____

Address _____
      Street or Box   City   State   Zip

Home Phone _____ Business Phone _____

Occupation (Student, etc.) _____

Experience with Disabled People _____

Skiing Level (Beginner, Intermediate, Advanced) _____

In Case of Emergency Contact _____

Program:

_____ Weekly Programs _____
                              Day

_____ Special Groups _____ _____
                   Weekend   Weekday

_____ Sleds _____ _____
                 Weekend   Weekday

Place of Employment _____

Address _____

_____

APPLICANT MUST BE 18 YEARS OF AGE TO VOLUNTEER.

This form is used principally for groups coming from schools or centers. It provides information on both the individual and the sponsoring group and identifies a responsible person to contact.

Special Populations Information

Name _____

Address _____ City _____

State _____ Zip _____ Phone _____

School or Center _____

Address _____ City _____

State _____ Zip _____ Phone _____

Age _____ Sex _____ Height _____ Weight _____

In case of emergency contact _____ Phone _____

Applicant's Physician _____ Phone _____

Disability _____

Subject to seizures? _____ Controlled by medication _____

Number of years/months since last seizure _____

Special instructions relative to seizures _____

_____

Person responsible for choosing applicant _____

Summer _____ Winter _____ Year _____

_____
Signature of person filling out card

Participant's attendance record for Winter Park staff use

Date								
Attendance								

This form can be used in grant proposal writing and other fundraising efforts to show program purposes and populations served.

To obtain government grants and various other funds which are needed for the continued success of the Winter Park Handicap Program, we request that you provide us with the following statistics:

This information is voluntary. Please do not list your name.

Please check the appropriate boxes —

Race/Ethnic Origin

- ☐ Hispanic
- ☐ Asian or Pacific Islander
- ☐ American Indian
- ☐ Black
- ☐ White
- ☐ Other

Family Income

- ☐ Under $10,000
- ☐ $10,000 to $20,000
- ☐ $20,000 to $30,000
- ☐ $30,000 to $40,000
- ☐ $40,000 to $50,000
- ☐ Over $50,000

This form is used in duplicate to register equipment rental. The student keeps one copy, the equipment room the other.

Winter Park Sports and Learning Center

Name _____ Last _____ First _____ Center _____ (If applicable)

Address _____ Date _____

City _____ State _____ Zip _____

Disability _____ Age _____ Sex _____

Shoe Size _____ Height _____ ft. _____ in. Weight _____ lbs.

Skiing Ability (circle one)   Beginner   Intermediate   Expert

Binding Setting

Toe	Heel	Tech. In.

Poles _____ Boot # _____ Ski # _____ Outrigger # _____

Adaptive _____

ALL EQUIPMENT MUST BE RETURNED BY 4:00 P.M.

I understand skiing is a sport which involves a certain amount of risk, which can be minimized but not eliminated by the use of good equipment that is properly adjusted. I verify that the binding release indicators correspond to the numbers written above. I understand that if my equipment is lost or stolen, I am solely responsible to pay the replacement cost at retail value. I have read and understand the preceding agreement.

_____

Signature of Responsible Party

This form keeps track of the volunteer instructors' working record for compliance with requirements.

Instructor Information Forms

Program _____

Coordinator _____

Instructor Information

Name _____

Address _____

Phone _____

Instructor Attendance Record

Date												
Worked												
Late												

Instructor Performance Evaluation

Attitude

Teaching Ability

This form serves as a report card on the student's progress.

Winter Park Sports and Learning Center

Student _____

Agency _____

Instructor _____

Date	X		Date	X	
		Equipment			Introduction to Poles
		Walking			Advanced Wide Track Parallel
		Step Around			Moguls
		Falling			Racing
		Getting Up			**Slopes**
		Body Position			Mt. Maury _____
		Straight Run			Turnpike _____
		Gliding Wedge			Kendrick _____
		Stop			Phipps _____
		Controlled Wedge			Practice _____
		Turn to Stop, Both Directions			_____
		Linked Turns			_____
		Beginning Wide Track Parallel			_____

Comments:

This Memorandum defines line cutting policy for disabled skiers.

MEMORANDUM

TO: All Lift Department and Handicap Program Employees

FROM: Hal O'Leary

SUBJECT: LINE CUTTING POLICY FOR THE HANDICAPPED

In an effort to help reduce the number of people cutting lift lines, the following restrictions will apply:

1. The following instructors of the handicapped will be permitted to cut lift lines with a ticketed student:
   — Full time employees wearing a Winter Park Resort uniform coat;
   — Interns wearing a Winter Park Resort uniform coat;
   — Volunteers working on Saturdays and Sundays wearing a red leg gator with insignia. (Volunteers working Monday through Friday must wait in the lift line with their students.)

2. The following handicapped individuals will be permitted to cut lift lines:
   — Above-the-knee amputees with one ticketed guest;
   — Below-the-knee amputees skiing on one ski, with one ticketed guest;
   — Four track skiers with two skis and two outriggers, with one ticketed guest;
   — Spinal cord injured using the mono-ski or sit ski with a trained tetherer and one ticketed aide;
   — Blind skiers with orange bibs with one instructor wearing an orange bib.

"Our heartfelt thanks and gratitude not only for the satisfaction our daughter had in learning the skills of skiing but also for the people who have touched her life."

This back-to-back form is used with the individual student to develop necessary information and to track progress.

Winter Park Handicap Ski Program

Name _____ Address _____

City _____ State _____ Zip _____ Phone _____

Date of Birth _____ Parents' Name (If Under 21) _____

Parents' Address _____ City _____ State _____ Zip _____

Disability _____

Place of Employment _____ Address _____

City _____ State _____ Zip _____ Position _____

In which other sports do you participate? _____

_____

Family Recreational Activities _____

Usual Mode of Transportation to Winter Park _____

How many people accompanied you? _____ Family Members _____ Friends _____

Do you stay overnight in Winter Park? _____ Where? _____

Usual length of stay _____ _____

Have you encountered physical barriers in accommodations? (Please specify) _____

_____

_____

What do you enjoy most about the ski program? _____

_____

Equipment _____

Medication _____

_____

_____

_____

DATE	PROGRESS

The Winter Park Handicapped Competition Program (WPHCP) had its beginnings in 1979. Under the direction of Handicap Program instructor Fred Tassone and Winter Park employee Homer Jennings, informal race training was offered to handicapped skiers eyeing the newly developing U.S. National Championship Series and the U.S. Disabled Ski Team (USDST), sponsored by the National Handicapped Sports and Recreation Association (NHSRA). In 1981 the program started to gel into a group of hard-core racers living in Winter Park and training, while holding part-time jobs around town. Winter Park Resort was fast becoming the unofficial home of the USDST. Racers in the program were starting to make their mark in national and international competition.

By 1984 the NHSRA had developed its National Championships to the point of having racers qualify through a regional race series, and the USDST had become a major power on the international race scene. To keep up with this increased level of competition, both NHSRA and Winter Park started looking at the possibility of expanding WPHCP into a full scale, structured, season-long training program serving not only the local racers, but also providing much needed training for developing racers around the country. In September of 1984, a proposal was submitted by USDST member Paul DiBello and accepted by Winter Park with the blessing of NHSRA. A program would be designed to offer handicapped ski racers structured training time in both a full season and camp format similar to those offered to all skiers throughout the world.

WPHCP is now a firmly established, high level training program for over 200 racers around the country, and remains a key developmental training program for skiers seeking their personal best.

"When they are on the slopes, they are on the same level as all the other skiers and looked up to by many as having the courage to attempt to ski, let alone compete."

*Paul DiBello
Program Director*

Absorbing — Flexing to take pressure in the joints.

Angulation — Limited sideways bending in areas of flex.

Braquage — The action of turning both legs simultaneously in the same direction.

Christie — Skidding or sliding motion.

Christie Turn — The maneuver in which both skis are turning and skidding on corresponding edges during the arc of the turn.

Controlled Skid — The total result of the skis rotating while moving forward and at an angle. Can be controlled by varying degrees of applied pressure according to the requirement of the maneuver.

Edge Control — The action of adjusting or tilting the edge of the ski according to the desired maneuver.

Equalizing the Arc — Repeating in both directions an identical arc by simultaneously steering both skis, utilizing equal pressure control and rotary movements.

Fall Line — Imaginary path a round object would take down the hill.

Flex — Maintaining proper body position by bending of the ankles, knees and hips which prevents a static position, permitting the individual to adjust to changing terrain.

Four Track — Two skis and two outriggers.

Hockey Stop — Simultaneous turning of the skis abruptly while using forward pressure and edge control to a sudden stop.

Hop Turn — Utilized solely by the three track skier. Introduced as a beginning maneuver to change direction and to familiarize the student with his equipment. Also assists in changing direction during the beginning traverse phase.

Inclination/ Banking — The degree of a slant; if uphill, it's called ''banking''.

Outrun — Unobstructed natural run-out of the terrain which allows student to come to a full stop.

Pole Plant — Initiates the beginning of a turn and encourages rhythm, edge control and weight shift.

| # Skiing Terminology

Pressure Applying weight; it can be to the edges of the skis, from one ski to the other (weight transfer); from one end of the ski to other end; in walking and climbing maneuvers, etc.

Short Swing Linked short radius turns utilizing anticipation and pivoted rebound.

Side Stepping Means of climbing hill in beginning phases by having skis perpendicular to fall line and utilizing uphill edge of ski.

Straight Run Skis placed in a wide track parallel position with equal pressure on both skis, emphasizing proper body position.

Tetherer An individual who skis behind the sit ski using a tether line which is attached to the sit ski for safety purposes.

Three Track One ski and two outriggers.

Touch System Used to assist students to assume a proper ski position by touching the knees, hips, etc.

Traverse Sliding in a direction which deviates from the fall line.

Two Point Hold Accomplished by using the following steps:

1. Work from behind the student;
2. The instructor positions one ski between the student's skis and the other ski on the outside;
3. Place the outside hand below the knee of the student and the other hand on the student's shoulder or hip, depending on which feels more comfortable for instructional purposes.

For disabled individuals, the two point hold position can serve as an important tool in teaching control, assisting in turning and in stopping. This maneuver should eventually lead to the student becoming independent of the instructor.

Uphill Christie Simultaneous steering of both skis into the hill while skidding to a complete stop.

Wedge Equal displacement of the tails of the skis, forming a "piece of pie."

Weighting/ Unweighting Pressure control to achieve weight transfer

Wide Track Parallel Turns Simultaneous steering of both skis followed by the rotation of the legs and skidding of the skis. Skier assumes parallel stance throughout the progression of the turn.

Arthritis | The term arthritis means inflammation of a joint.

The clinical picture is usually that of single or multiple joint involvement with symptoms of pain, swelling, stiffness and heat (redness) in the joint(s), and fever and malaise (discomfort — often indicative of infection) in the individual. With arthritis, the inflammation itself is damaging to tissue, causing muscle wasting, loss of range of motion, joint destruction and eventually deformity.

Most major forms of arthritis are chronic conditions, meaning that once started, they continue for life in most individuals. Nearly all individuals with arthritis may have remission periods, when the disease seems to have disappeared completely. During the remissions, the individual with arthritis may feel perfectly well while x-ray and blood tests reveal that the arthritis is still active but at a lesser degree. A ``flare-up'' is the terminology used to describe the period of time that the disease is in a very active form.

The five most widespread kinds of arthritis, with explanations of how they are different, are:

Rheumatoid Arthritis: This is the most serious, the most painful, the most crippling. Inflammatory and chronic, it can affect the whole body. Primarily it attacks the joints, but it can also cause disease in the lungs, skin, blood vessels, muscles, spleen, heart, and even the eyes. In children it occurs in a form known as juvenile rheumatoid arthritis.

Osteoarthritis: Also called degenerative joint disease, this is principally a wear-and-tear disease of the joints which comes with getting older. It is usually mild and is not generally inflammatory. It does not cause general illness. Sometimes there can be considerable pain. Mild to severe disability may develop gradually.

Ankylosing Spondylitis: This is chronic inflammatory arthritis of the spine. It affects men ten times as often as women, usually beginning in the teens or early twenties.

Rheumatic Fever: This is an acute disease which follows a streptococcus infection. It frequently damages the heart. It also causes arthritis which usually subsides quickly without crippling.

Gout: Also called gouty arthritis, this is an inherited disease which most often attacks small joints, especially the big toe. Most victims are men. It is intensely painful.

The exact cause of arthritis is unknown. Two theories have been suggested but have not been proven through research.

Arthritis may be caused by a virus. Present research has not been able to prove definitely that any germ is responsible for the disease.

Many experts think that arthritis may be caused by an imbalance of the body's own defense or immunity mechanism: that complicated body chemistry is thrown out of balance so that the body produces antibodies which attack its own joints and tissues.

Arthritis is seen more often in women than men in a ratio of about 2 to 1. Hereditary factors have been suspected since some families demonstrate multiple cases. It is most likely to affect people between ages 20 to 50, but can occur at any age.

"The instructors never fail to amaze me with their knowledge of disabilities and ski modifications necessary to motivate these kids."

Cancer: Leukemia and sarcoma

Cancer is characterized by abnormal and uncontrolled growth of cells. Cells are tiny structures that make up all parts of the body. All cells reproduce themselves by dividing. Normal growth and repair of tissue take place in this orderly manner.

When cell division is not orderly and controlled, abnormal growth occurs. A mass of tissue called a tumor builds up. A tumor may be benign or malignant. A malignant tumor is a cancer.

Leukemia is a cancer of the bone marrow. The bone marrow is the spongy tissue filling the center core of bones and the source of the body's blood. Sarcoma is a cancer of the connective tissue.

A malignant tumor, or cancer, invades neighboring tissues and organs and can spread to other parts of the body, forming new growths called metastases. If cancer cells have spread before a tumor is removed, the disease can recur.

The three main methods of treating cancer are: (1) surgery, (2) radiation therapy, and (3) chemotherapy (treatment with anticancer drugs). In many cases treatment consists of two or all three of these methods, a procedure called combination therapy. Both leukemia and sarcoma are treated with chemotherapy.

Anticancer drugs can kill cancer cells in most parts of the body but can also act on normal cells. Even though children in such treatment may look healthy, be aware that they may be more tired, more apt to bruise and hurt, develop infections and become weak. They may be depressed and have an altered mood. There may be partial or total hair loss, the blood count may drop below normal, and resistance to infection may be lowered. Some patients undergoing chemotherapy experience diarrhea, nausea, vomiting and loss of appetite. Small ulcers may form in the mouth.

Caution should be taken with different types of sarcoma surgery (amputation of extremities). The amputation may still have a tumor, making a fracture in that area a possibility.

Cerebral Palsy

Cerebral Palsy is a term that describes any disorder of movement and posture that results from a non-progressive abnormality of the immature brain. Damage to the brain may occur before birth, during delivery or immediately after birth — usually as a result of deprivation of oxygen to the brain. The condition of cerebral palsy can also occur in young children who sustain trauma and resultant injury of the brain.

The brain is the control center from which all body function, thoughts, and psychological processes are controlled. Different areas of the brain control different functions: i.e., movement, speech, learning, judgment, hearing, vision, emotions, to name only a few. The area and degree of damage to the brain determine the resultant disability. Often, in addition to damage to the movement area of the brain, other areas are affected. Therefore, more than one of the functions previously listed may be affected in the individual with cerebral palsy. In all cases, the characteristics of abnormal muscle tone, a delay in normal development and abnormal reflex activity are seen.

Physically, cerebral palsy is classified as one or a combination of the following: (1) spastic (tense, contracted muscles); (2) athetoid (extraneous, uncontrolled movements); (3) ataxic (jerky, uncontrolled movements); (4) rigid (stiff, uncontrolled movements); and (5) flaccid (reduced, diminished muscle tone). These vary in degree or severity, from the minimally involved individual, who can function without much evidence of abnormal movement, to the severely involved individual, who has minimal active muscle control and is noted to be controlled by significant abnormal muscle tone.

Cerebral palsy is a life-long condition that does not get worse except by the general aging process that everyone experiences.

Management for cerebral palsy often includes physical therapy, occupational therapy, speech therapy, medication, orthopedic management of surgery and/or bracing, and other special aids such as wheelchairs, adaptive aids, hearing aids, and so forth.

As with other neurological disorders, learning disabilities, social immaturity, and emotional needs can play an important part in the overall management of each person with cerebral palsy. Communication at an effective level is critical.

Generally speaking, instability is a significant factor in limiting functional movement in cerebral palsy. Abnormal postures and positioning are heightened with higher level and more stressful physical activities. Abnormal patterns should not be reinforced. Instead, adapt the activity to provide the needed stability in order to gain success in movement.

Susan Hildebrecht

Developmental Disabilities

The population of persons with developmental disabilities living in the United States is estimated to be about ten million. Their disabilities are caused by physical and mental impairments which are chronic and severe and have occurred during the growth and developmental period of their lives. The most commonly known conditions which fall under the category of developmental disabilities are mental retardation, cerebral palsy, autism, epilepsy and Down's syndrome.

Mental Retardation

By definition, a mentally retarded person is one who, from childhood, develops at a below average rate and experiences difficulty in learning, social adjustment and economic productivity.

"Our ski kids have all shown improvement, especially in their social relationships, sportsmanship skills, language processing skills, and in their own more positive self concepts."

The vast majority are classified as mildly retarded. They differ from non-retarded people only in the rate and degree of intellectual development. In fact, their retardation is not usually apparent until they enter school. And then, as adults, they often lose their identity as retarded when they enter the job market and daily community life.

Moderately retarded persons usually show their developmental delay before they reach school age. However, appropriate community-based education throughout their developmental years can prepare these people to live a satisfying and productive life in the community.

Severely and profoundly retarded persons show the most pronounced developmental problems and frequently have handicaps in addition to mental retardation. Systematic training efforts have proven that, with very few exceptions, severely and profoundly retarded persons can learn to care for their basic needs. Many also can perform useful work activities, with supervision, and can otherwise adapt to normal patterns of life.

Any condition that hinders or interferes with intellectual development before or during birth or in the early childhood years can be the cause of mental retardation. And although more than 250 causes are known, these account for only one fourth of all identified cases.

Among the well-known causes are: German measles in the mother during the first three months of pregnancy, syphillis, meningitis, toxoplasmosis, Rh-factor incompatibility between mother and infant, malnutrition and chromosome abnormalities, such as Down's syndrome.

Undoubtedly, among the mildly retarded there are many whose development has been adversely affected by things like inadequate diet, poor prenatal care and lack of learning opportunities. Infants and young children need the right kind of mental activity just as they need the right kind of physical activity. And when this activity is lacking, delays can occur. So these early years, when the nervous system is maturing and language is developing, are very critical.

Destruction of brain tissue or interference with brain development in babies or small children frequently produces mental retardation. This accounts for a large number of cases of moderate, severe and profound mental retardation. We can't be sure to what degree brain damage contributes in cases of mild retardation, and expert opinion is divided.

Down's syndrome

Down's syndrome is a combination of birth defects including mental retardation. The child with Down's syndrome may have oval-shaped eyes, a tongue that seems big for the mouth, and a short neck. The child or adult is usually short in stature and has unusual looseness of the joints.

The degree of mental retardation varies widely, from mild to moderate to severe. There is no way to predict the mental development of a child with Down's syndrome from the physical appearance.

Many of those with Down's syndrome have heart abnormalities and frequently, surgery can correct these problems. A child with Down's syndrome may have many colds, bronchitis and pneumonia. These children, like all others, should receive regular medical care including eye and hearing tests as well as regular immunizations.

Pat Campanello and Hal with a happy first-day skier with Down's syndrome.　PHOTO: R.J. WALKER

A baby is formed when the egg from the mother and the sperm from the father come together. Normally, egg and sperm cells each have 23 chromosomes. Chromosomes are the hereditary information packets of every living cell. In the usual case of a child with Down's syndrome, either the egg or the sperm cell contributes 24 chromosomes, instead of 23. The result is that the chromosomes present total 47, instead of the normal 46. The extra chromosome causes the mental and physical characteristics of Down's syndrome.

Autism

Autism is a severely incapacitating, lifelong developmental disability that usually appears during the first three years of life. Autism is four times more common in males than females and has been found throughout the world in families of all racial, ethnic and social backgrounds.

The symptoms of autism include:
— Slow development or lack of physical, social and learning skills.
— Immature rhythms of speech, limited understanding of ideas, and use of words without attaching the usual meaning to them.
— Abnormal responses to sensations. Sight, hearing, touch, pain, balance, smell, taste, the way a child holds his body — any one of a combination of these responses may be affected.
— Abnormal ways of relating to people, objects and events.

In IQ testing, approximately 60% of autistic patients have scores below 50, 20% between 50 and 70, and 20% greater than 70. Most patients show wide variations in performance on different tests at different times. Many autistic children have distinct skills in music, mathematics, or in using spatial concepts (for example, working jigsaw puzzles), but are severely retarded in other areas.

There appear to be several causes of autism, each with distinct neurological effects. No known factors in the psychological environment of a child have been shown to cause autism.

Autism occurs either by itself or in association with other disorders which affect brain function. Perinatal viral infections, some metabolic disturbances, epilepsy or mental retardation may result in autistic behavior.

Severe autism may cause extreme forms of self-injurious, repetitive, highly unusual and aggressive behavior. The behavior may persist and be very difficult to change, posing a tremendous challenge to those who must manage, treat and teach autistic people. In its milder form, autism most resembles a learning disability such as childhood aphasia. Usually, however, people with autism are substantially handicapped.

Various methods of treatment have been tried but no single treatment is effective in all cases. There is no cure in a medical sense.

Epilepsy Epilepsy is a physical condition that happens when there are sudden, brief changes in how the brain works. When brain cells are not working properly, a person's consciousness, movements or actions may be changed for a short time. These physical changes are called epileptic seizures. Epilepsy is therefore sometimes called a seizure disorder. Epilepsy affects people in all nations and of all races.

In about half of all cases there is no one cause that can be found. Among the rest, epilepsy may be caused by any one of a number of things that make a difference in the way the brain works. For example, head injuries or lack of oxygen during birth may damage the delicate electrical system in the brain. Other causes include brain tumors, genetic conditions (such as tuberous sclerosis), lead poisoning, problems in development of the brain before birth, illnesses like meningitis, encephalitis, or even severe cases of measles.

The brain is the control center for the body. Normal electrical signals between cells make the brain and body work correctly. The cells work like little switches, turning electrical charges on and off automatically. But sometimes it is as if some cells get stuck in the ''on'' position. The extra energy they produce affects other cells and spreads to other parts or through all of the brain. This extra energy blocks out our usual awareness of things around us, or may change the way the world looks, or may make our bodies move automatically. Sometimes it may cause a convulsion. These seizures usually last a short time (a matter of seconds or two to three minutes), and then end naturally as special chemicals in the brain bring cell activity back to normal.

Seizures can be of two major types — convulsive or non-convulsive. A convulsive seizure (also called grand mal) happens when the whole brain is suddenly swamped with extra electrical energy. It often starts with a hoarse cry caused by air being suddenly forced out of the lungs. The person falls to the ground unconscious. The body stiffens briefly, and then begins jerking movements.

Bladder or bowel control is sometimes lost. The tongue may be bitten. A frothy saliva may appear around the mouth, caused by air being forced through mouth fluids. Breathing may get very shallow and even stop for a few moments. Sometimes the skin turns a bluish color because the lower rate of breathing is supplying less oxygen than usual. The jerking movements then slow down, and the seizure ends naturally after a minute or two. After returning to consciousness the person may feel confused and sleepy. In some cases only a very short recovery period is required, and most people can go back to their normal activities after resting for a while.

Diabetes

Diabetes is a disease in which the ability to use/burn carbohydrates (sugar) works improperly. The body of an individual who has diabetes is unable to burn up the carbohydrates because of a lack of insulin, which is produced by the pancreas. The lack of insulin in the blood prevents the storage of glucose (the body's gasoline) in the cells of the liver. Consequently, blood sugar accumulates in the blood stream in greater than usual amounts.

Signs of diabetes may include a general lack of energy, frequent urination, excessive thirst, and a sudden loss of weight. Overweight is a common characteristic of individuals with diabetes, particularly in adults. Reducing to a normal weight often brings about definite improvement in the diabetic condition. The individual with diabetes is more susceptible to infection; thus care and proper treatment must be used in the event that blisters, cuts, scratches or infections occur. The control of diabetes is done through diet and medication. If injections are necessary, the individual usually does this. If shots are used to control the diabetes, they usually are taken once or twice daily, depending upon the individual's needs and the type of insulin used. Diabetes can't be cured but it can be controlled. The individual with diabetes can live as long and as productive a life as other people.

The most serious characteristic of diabetes is called "insulin shock." This condition occurs when the sugar stored in the liver is gone. The individual develops general muscle weakness, mental confusion, dizziness, heavy sweating, trembling, and either pale or flushed face. A too large dose of insulin can bring about a more rapid reaction. When warning signs appear, the individual should eat or drink something with sugar in it (candy bar, coke, orange juice, etc.). If the individual doesn't get enough insulin at one time, weakness, weariness, loss of appetite, nausea, thirst and urination are signs. If this occurs, the person should take another shot of insulin.

Friedreich's Ataxia

Friedreich's Ataxia is a genetic disorder resulting in progressive deterioration of the nervous system, causing an inability to coordinate voluntary muscle movement. Intelligence and the special senses are usually unimpaired.

The disorder usually begins between the ages of 10 and 13, starting with an unsteadiness in the legs. Over a period of eight to ten years, the individual will lose the ability to walk unassisted. This condition is often associated with fatigue, total absence of tendon reflexes, weakness and loss of coordinated arm and hand movement resulting in difficulty with manipulative tasks. The individual is very dependent upon visual cues for motor function. It is known that the disorder is inherited. No cure has been developed for Friedreich's Ataxia. Medical management is dictated by the individual's needs as they develop. Some individuals need to wear braces or use wheelchairs or other adaptive devices that will assist the individual in being independent. As the disorder progresses, deformities will occur, especially in the spinal column and feet. The individual will experience difficulty with speech. The heart muscle can also be affected.

Head Injury

A head injury is a traumatic insult to the brain; although this injury is not always visible, it may cause physical, intellectual, emotional, social and vocational changes. These changes affect not only the present but future status of an individual. Indeed, it frequently means that the person may never quite be the same again. Although no visible damage is noted, the psychological and intellectual consequences of a head injury can be devastating to that person and to those who are close to the individual.

This first category is known as "closed head injury." Its cause is often a rapid acceleration/deceleration (whereby the brain is whipped back and forth in quick motion) that occurs in motor vehicle accidents. This pull and tug places extreme stress on the brain stem — the part that connects the larger part of the brain with the spinal cord and the rest of the body. A large number of functions are packed tightly in the brain stem, i.e. controls of consciousness, breathing, heart beat, eye movements, pupil reactions, swallowing and facial movements. Furthermore, all sensations going to the brain, as well as signals from the brain to the muscles, must pass through the brain stem. The stress of rapid deceleration pulls apart nerve fibers and causes damage to the activated system of neuro-fibers which send out these important messages to all parts of the body.

The second category of Head Injury is usually referred to as "open head injury." This is a visible assault and may be the result of an accident, gun shot wound or a variety of other out-side factors. A head injury also may occur following cardiac arrest, stroke or accident, such as drowning and many other causes due to loss of oxygen to the brain. Symptoms can vary greatly and are unique, depending on the extent and location of the brain injury. Physical disabilities, impaired learning ability and personality changes are common.

1. Physical Impairments: speech, vision, hearing and other sensory impairments, headaches, lack of coordination, spasticity of muscles, paralysis of one or both sides and seizure disorders.

2. Cognitive Impairments: memory deficits — short and long term concentration, slowness of thinking, attention, perception, communication, reading and writing skills, planning, sequencing and judgment.

3. Psycho-Social-Behavioral-Emotional Impairments: fatigue, mood swings, denial, self-centeredness, anxiety, depression, lowered self-esteem, sexual dysfunction, restlessness, lack of motivation, inability to self-monitor, difficulty with emotional control, inability to cope, agitation, excessive laughing or crying and difficulty in relation to others.

Any or all of the above impairments may occur in different degrees, and there may be other symptoms not listed above. It is important to note that with *early* and ongoing therapeutic intervention, the severity of these symptoms might decrease. Intellectual ability might *not* improve after a period of time, but social and behavioral aspects and memory could improve over a long period of time.

Anatomy of the Brain

The brain is divided into two halves, or *hemispheres* which have specialized functions. The left hemisphere controls movement and perceives touch on the right side of the body. It is the center for logic and verbal ability (language comprehension, speaking, reading, and writing). The right hemisphere controls the left side of the body and deals with spatial orientation; the ability to judge distance, shape, form and body position in space. The right hemisphere is more creative, intuitive and important for music and art appreciation. The outer covering of the brain, or *cortex* controls all of our conscious activity, including thoughts, movements, feelings, speech, emotions, judgments, and memories.

Right Hemisphere

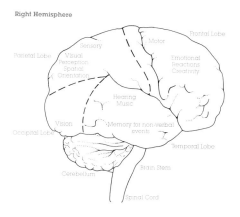

Left Hemisphere

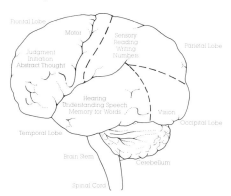

The *brain stem* is at the base of the cerebral hemispheres and connects the spinal cord and the cortex. Nerve tracts carrying information to the cortex (*sensory*) and from the cortex (*motor*) pass through the brain stem. The brain stem contains centers which automatically regulate wakefulness and sleep, breathing, and heart action. *Cranial nerves* travel from the brain stem to all parts of the face and neck to move muscles of the face, eyes, lips, tongue and voice. Smells, sight, and sound are transmitted through the cranial nerves to the cortex.

The *cerebellum* is behind the brain stem and controls muscle coordination. Motor movements, such as walking, talking, and writing are smooth and coordinated from regulation by the cerebellum.

Deep in the brain are four cavities called *ventricles* filled with clear liquid (*cerebrospinal fluid*). These four ventricles and the spinal cord are all connected by narrow passageways. The fluid travels from ventricle to ventricle and all along the spinal cord. The purpose of cerebrospinal fluid is to cushion the brain.

Brain damage occurs when brain cells are deprived of oxygen. Direct trauma to the head, cardiac arrest, respiratory arrest, or blood clots in the brain can all cause brain cells to die from lack of oxygen. Once a brain cell is destroyed, it cannot be regenerated. The symptoms that result from brain injury are varied and depend on the areas of the brain that have been damaged.

Right Hemiplegia

The person who has sustained damage to the left side of the brain, resulting in right-sided paralysis, is referred to as a right hemiplegic. Since speech and language are also controlled by the left side of the brain, the right hemiplegic is likely to have difficulties with speech and/or language.

Speech refers to the way sounds and words are formed by the coordination of breathing, voice, movement of the mouth, lips and tongue. When there is muscle weakness, paralysis, and/or incoordination, speech will be distorted, slurred and difficult to understand. This is known as *dysarthria*.

Language refers to the way we learn words and their meanings and how we put them together to form sentences. We use language to communicate through talking, writing, reading and listening. Loss of this ability to use language is called *aphasia*. A patient with aphasia may have difficulty understanding or producing any form of language. What he hears or reads may be meaningless. He may be unable to think of the words he wants to say. His speech may not always be meaningful or express a complete thought. Writing is usually not an alternative to speaking as most aphasics have just as much difficulty trying to write words as they do saying them.

When communicating with an aphasic person, it is helpful to use both words and gestures to help him understand what you are talking about. Use short, simple sentences but do not "talk down'' to him. Speak in a normal tone of voice. Aphasics are not deaf but merely have difficulty understanding the meaning of the words they hear. Try to ask questions which do not require a choice. ''Do you want to go to bed?'' is better than ''Do you want to go to bed or stay up and watch TV?'' Give the person time to answer as best he can before continuing on to another question. If the person cannot think of the word, encourage him to show you what he needs. The patient's speech pathologist can give you specific suggestions for the best means of communicating with him.

Loss of language does not mean the person is less intelligent. Having aphasia is a bit like trying to communicate in a foreign country when you can only say or understand a few words of the language.

At times an aphasic may laugh or cry more easily and inappropriately. This is due to *lability* which is lack of emotional control. Excessive or unexpected swearing may be present.

A person with right hemiplegia may also have a visual field cut which means he cannot see on his right side. He must learn to turn his head until he sees a whole object. If this condition is present, try to approach the person from the left and keep things he needs on his good side.

Left Hemiplegia   The patient referred to as a left hemiplegic or left hemi has experienced damage to the right hemisphere (right side) of his brain. The patient's left arm and/or leg may be paralyzed or weakened. There may also be paralysis or weakness of the left facial muscles.

Characteristically, the left hemi patient retains good understanding of spoken language, expresses himself adequately and has good memory for events prior to injury. However, there are other problems that the speech pathologist may assist the patient with. Memory for new materials presented and events since injury may be impaired. The patient may have difficulty with time and place concepts. He may be unable to relate one event to another. Performance on physical activities as well as reading and writing may be marked with inconsistency and distractibility. Some patients may repeat a thought or physical motion over and over. This is called *perseveration*.

The left hemiplegic patient may experience visual perceptual problems or *left aversion*. Understanding the visual relationship of one object to another, realizing his own body position in space, organizing and sequencing visual stimuli, and judging distances are typical visual perceptual problems a person with right hemisphere damage might experience. Left aversion or left ignoral refers to a patient's lack of awareness of his left side or the left side of objects. For example, he may bump into objects on his left side, comb only the right side of his hair, or eat food from just the right side of his plate.

Simple daily tasks, such as dressing and brushing the teeth, become difficult because of visual perceptual problems and the left aversion. Many left hemis have difficulty with reading, arithmetic, and writing because they miss words and numbers on the page. It is necessary to teach the patient to be more aware of his visual perceptual deficits through practice and frequent repetition in order for him to compensate for these problems.

Some patients experience personality or behavior changes. They may make excuses for their deficits. They may have less emotional control and become upset more easily (*lability*). Their ability for judgment, reasoning, problem solving, and logical thinking may be reduced. In such cases, supervision of daily activities may be necessary. Attempts to reason with the patient may be futile and may lead to an extended argument. This can be upsetting to the patient and the family.

Awareness and understanding are primary in helping the patient compensate for his problems. Tasks aimed at increasing attention span, requiring the patient to attend to the left side of objects, and fitting pieces together to make a whole are often helpful to the left hemiplegic. Frequent repetition and re-direction may be necessary.

Brain Injury   Following brain injury a number of communications problems may occur. A person may have any of these problems or any combination:

1. Decrease in level of awareness (cognitive functioning) or information processing skills.
2. Difficulty speaking due to paralysis, weakness and/or incoordination of the muscles used for speech, breath and voice.
3. Difficulty understanding what is heard or read (seen).
4. Difficulty recalling words for spoken or written language.
5. Difficulty with memory — past and present.
6. Problems with orientation of time, place, space or reality.

Shunts   Shunts, generally speaking, are devices to redirect the flow of fluids. With respect to the patient with brain injury, a shunt is a surgically implanted plastic tubing which redirects the flow of cerebrospinal fluid (CS.F). In certain situations, a shunt can prevent further brain injury when there is evidence of decreased re-absorption of CS.F by the brain covering.

Learning Disability   Persons who have a learning disability do not have mental retardation nor are they slow learners; rather, these individuals usually have average or above average intelligence. Additionally, there is usually no obvious physical disability, and this is why it is often referred to as a hidden disability.

An individual with a learning disability has difficulty with the messages to the brain becoming jumbled, thus making it difficult for the individual to learn in one or more of the academic areas; however they can learn and be successful as lawyers, doctors, social service workers, etc. They must learn to compensate for their difficulties by learning in ways which are different from the average way people learn.

"The instructor made our son, a child with learning disabilities, feel that he was finally able to be good at something."

As with many other disabilities, there is a variety of factors which may be responsible for a person having a learning disability and these may include:

Pre-natal — maternal malnutrition, toxemia in pregnancy, alcoholism during pregnancy, taking certain drugs, RH incompatibility, infectious/viral illness in the pregnant mother.

During birth — long difficult delivery, lack of oxygen, prematurity, dry birth, intracranial pressure (due to forceps delivery), a narrow pelvic arch in the mother or too rapid delivery.

After birth — delay in breathing, high fever at an early age, sharp blow to the head from a fall or accident, lead poisoning, drug intoxication, suffocation or breath holding or severe nutritional deficiencies. Here are some of the most common characteristics of a learning disability. A person with a learning disability will not show all of the characteristics, and a person who does not have a learning disability may also show some of the characteristics:

• short attention span/easily distracted

- difficulty in following instructions
- poor reasoning ability
- inability to set realistic goals by themselves
- poor reading ability/adds, omits words when reading
- difficulty distinguishing between p, g, k, d and q
- reads "on" for "no" "was" for "saw," etc.
- difficulty with concepts left, right, above, below, up, down, yesterday, tomorrow, in, out, etc.
- difficulty telling time
- difficulty writing/writes "41" for "14"
- poor hand-eye coordination
- clumsy/accident prone
- disorganized/loses things
- quick tempered/easily irritated
- impulsive/gets caught up in details
- childish and bossy behavior
- needs constant recognition
- usually a loner

Multiple Sclerosis

Multiple sclerosis is a disease of the brain and spinal cord (the central nervous system). MS interferes with the brain's ability to control such functions as seeing, walking, talking, etc. It's called "multiple" because many scattered areas of the brain and spinal cord are affected, and symptoms can be mild or severe, come and go unpredictably. It's called "sclerosis" because the disease involves hardened tissue in the damaged area of the brain and spinal cord. When scarring occurs, it interrupts the passage of impulses along the nerve fiber. MS affects the central nervous system by acting like a switchboard by sending out electrical messages along the nerves to various parts of the body. These messages control all our conscious and unconscious movements so messages don't get through correctly and go to the wrong parts of the body.

Depending on what area of the nervous system is affected, individuals will have different symptoms. They may include one or more of the following: weakness, tingling numbness, impaired sensation, lack of coordination, disturbances in equilibrium, double vision, involuntary rapid movement of eyes, slurred speech, tremor, stiffness or spasticity, weakness of arms and legs, and with more severe cases of MS, paralysis and impaired bladder and bowel function can occur.

Approximately two-thirds of the individuals who have MS experience their first symptoms between the ages of 20 and 40. MS is not inherited nor is it contagious. The specific cause of MS is unknown. It is commonly found in colder climates. Attempts have been made to link it to infections, nutritional deficiency, lead poisoning, intoxication, and allergic reactions.

Multiple sclerosis follows a progressive course of physical deterioration. After each time a new symptom occurs, the individual with MS may improve some medically, but he/she usually does not achieve the function he/she had previously. MS has been known to progress over several decades. Emotional stress and fatigue can sometimes be linked to a temporary worsening of symptoms. Heat and humidity can also take a temporary toll on the person.

At the present time there is no cure for MS but there is continuous research being done.

Lud Kaftan, multiple sclerosis

Muscular Dystrophy

Muscular Dystrophy is a progressive disease that attacks the muscles. The disease usually affects the center muscles first, and weakness occurs progressively. It is found in men more than women. Eventually the condition extends to practically all voluntary muscles of the body. Muscular Dystrophy is not considered fatal. There are four types of Muscular Dystrophy:

Pseudohypertrophic: Most common form; starts in childhood between the ages of 3 and 10. Fat replaces muscles. It progresses more rapidly than any other type of Muscular Dystrophy. It is considered to be hereditary in 35% of the individuals with Muscular Dystrophy.

Facioscopulohmeral: Second most common type; affects the face muscles, the shoulders, and the upper arms. Most common age is 3 to 15.

Juvenile: It begins in late childhood, in the teen years or early adulthood, has a progression that is slower.

Mixed Types: It is a mixture of the first three types. The beginning of the disease may occur between the ages of 30 and 58. This type is not inherited.

Here are some characteristics of Muscular dystrophy:

- Tendency to tire quickly.
- Loss of fine motor control.
- Progressive weakness, causing possible postural problems.
- Possible emotional problems.
- Tendency to become ill more easily.

Spina Bifida

Spina Bifida (also called myelomeningocele or meningomyelocele) is a birth defect of the spinal column and spinal cord. The defect occurs in the fetus in early pregnancy when the covering over the spinal cord forms a "sac like pouch" and the vertebra(e) does not completely form to enclose the spinal cord at the defect site. Nerves from the spinal cord may grow into this "sac like pouch" and affect the connection between the brain and the spinal cord and the area the spinal cord innervates. Different muscles are controlled by nerves that connect to the spinal cord at different levels. The amount of nerve involvement varies greatly from individual to individual, depending on deficit level. Although the defect most often is in the lower spine, it can occur at higher levels. The lower the level, the fewer number of nerves involved and therefore, the more lower-extremity function the individual will have. In some cases, not all of the nerves at a given level of the defect are affected. In these cases, the individual may have "spotty" muscle function from nerves originating below the defect site.

In higher defects, the individual often cannot walk due to paralysis of the lower extremities and poor muscle control of the trunk. These individuals may be confined to wheelchairs for mobility. In very low level defects, individuals may be able to walk without or with minimal bracing. A wide variety of function and bracing needs is noted between these extremes of defect levels. Bracing can provide the stability needed to allow the individual to stand when muscle power is unbalanced or weak. Muscle imbalances often contribute to deformities of the bones and joints of the lower extremities and the spine.

The spinal cord includes nervous tissue relating to touch, temperature, pain and pressure as well as muscle function. Therefore, these sensations may also be affected in areas innervated from or below the defect site. The amount of deficit is also affected by the amount of spinal cord that is actually damaged at the defect site. Presence of any skin problems can lead to infection and can often be slow to heal. Therefore, it is very important to take measures to protect the skin from problems such as increased pressure, pressure areas, frostbite, excessive heat or cold, etc. Swelling or edema in the lower extremities often is noted in spina bifida because of poor circulation. Thus, pressure areas from shoes and braces are of concern. Visual skin checks are of utmost importance in order to maintain healthy skin.

Larry Kunz, spina bifida, four track racer and National Champion.
PHOTO: STEVE STONE

FINISH

Spinal fluid normally passes between 1) small blood vessels around the brain, 2) the spinal canal (in the center of the spinal cord), and 3) the ventricles in the center of the brain. Often the balance between the absorption of this fluid by the blood vessels is affected by the spinal defect of the spina bifida individual. If this occurs, it is called hydrocephalus. This creates increased spinal fluid pressure on the brain and brain damage could occur. In order to treat increased pressure caused by hydrocephalus, a shunting mechanism can be surgically implanted between the brain and the abdomen or heart where the fluid can be reabsorbed. The shunting mechanism is often identified by a prominence under the skin behind the ear and the prominence of a small tube running under the surface of the skin down the side of the neck and across the chest. Care must be taken to prevent direct blows to the side of the head where the shunt is located.

Nerves that control voluntary urination and defecation come from the lower portion of the spinal cord. This control is often affected in the individual with myelomeningocele. Urinary control by means of manual emptying of the bladder by pressure on the abdomen (Crede method) or use of a catheter to collect or create voiding may be used. A regular voiding program is necessary to prevent bladder and kidney infections as well as excessive back pressure on the kidneys. Bowels are usually managed through careful diets and when necessary, manual stimulation to the muscles controlling voiding and/or medication. Unexpected bladder or bowel voiding has been noted on occasion with increased physical activity or other forms of stimulation.

Many spina bifida individuals who do not walk or place very little stress on the lower extremities, as with standing, develop weakened bony structures which are more susceptible to fracture. This is particularly true in the long bones of the lower extremities and caution should be taken accordingly.

It is especially important to note that many spina bifida individuals, as well as those with other neurological problems, have learning problems and require special consideration. Evaluation of the individual's learning style and using this as a guideline in working with him/her are essential.

In conclusion, the individual with spina bifida has a complexity of characteristics involved with this defect. An understanding of his/her abilities and knowledge of the special precautions which must be taken are very important for those working with individuals who have spina bifida.

Spinal Cord Injury *Etiology and Incidence*

In the United States, there are over 150,000 people with spinal cord injury. The incidence is 25-35 new cases per 100,000 people annually. Recent data from the Spinal Cord Injury National Data Bank in Phoenix, Arizona, covering 3,123 Spinal Cord Injury (SCI) patients, revealed the following causes of injury: 36%, motor vehicle accidents; 16%, falls; 13%, gunshot wounds; 10%, diving; 6%, motorcycle accidents; 5%, falling objects and the remaining percentages divided into various other causes including sporting activities, medical/surgical complications and stab wounds. Snow skiing accounted for only 0.26% of the injuries.

Of these patients, 82% are male and 18% female. The age distribution is as follows: 0-14 years, 5%, 15-29 years, 62%; 30-44 years, 20%; 45-59 years, 10%; and greater than 60 years, 3%.

From this data, it can be seen that the majority of persons with SCI are young, active males, often interested in continuing an active lifestyle after their SCI. One of these active endeavors is skiing.

Make-up of the Nervous System

The central nervous system (CNS) is composed of the brain, spinal cord and spinal nerves, (Fig. 1). The spinal cord is an extension of the brain and is a cylindrical structure that is composed of nerve cells and fibers. Spinal nerves arise from the spinal cord and connect your brain with your muscles, skin and internal organs. When the CNS is intact, it is an extremely efficient communication system between brain and muscles, etc. The spinal cord sits in between these two areas acting much like a telephone line and communicating two way messages.

Emanating from the spinal cord, 31 pairs of spinal nerves branch out and connect to all parts of the body at various levels. Spinal nerves from the upper part of the cord connect with the upper part of the torso, arms and hands. Spinal nerves from the lower part of the cord connect with lower torso, pelvis, thighs, calves and feet.

Branching and dividing even further from the spinal cord are the peripheral nerves which reach every millimeter of your skin surface, every muscle, every blood vessel and every bone.

Figure 1

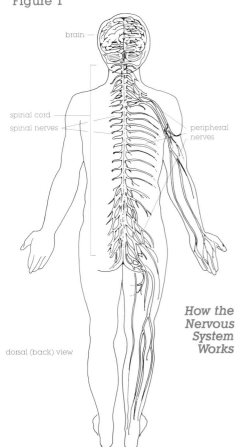

brain

spinal cord
spinal nerves

peripheral nerves

dorsal (back) view

How the Nervous System Works

Muscle movement begins in the brain and electrical impulses descend through the lateral and anterior parts of the spinal cord to the spinal nerves and out to the muscles. This is termed the motor pathway. When this pathway is injured, the result is paralysis or the inability to move muscles.

Sensation occurs when impulses travel from the skin or organs through the spinal nerves and ascend up the posterior and anterior/lateral parts of the spinal cord to the brain. This is termed the sensory pathway. When this pathway is injured, the result is loss of sensation. The type of motor/sensory loss a person has with a SCI depends on what areas of the spinal cord were damaged.

Anatomy

The spinal cord is protected by multiple bony structures called vertebrae which compose the spinal column commonly known as the "back bone." The spinal canal runs through the center of these vertebrae, and the spinal cord is located in this canal, (Fig. 2).

Figure 2

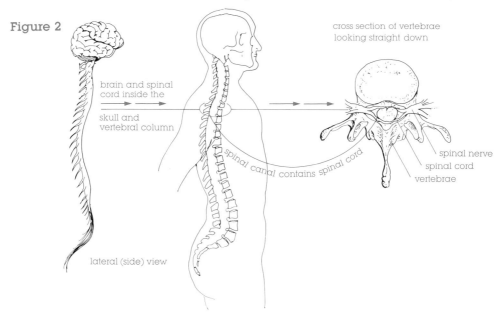

cross section of vertebrae looking straight down

brain and spinal cord inside the

skull and vertebral column

spinal canal contains spinal cord

spinal nerve
spinal cord
vertebrae

lateral (side) view

There are four major divisions of the spinal column: (Fig. 3)

1. The cervical region, or neck;

2. The thoracic region, or chest;

3. The lumbar region, or lower back;

4. The sacral region, or tail bone;

The cervical region contains the first seven vertebrae and the first eight spinal nerves.

The thoracic region is composed of the next twelve vertebrae and the next twelve spinal nerves.

The next five vertebrae and spinal nerves make up the lumbar region.

The last section of the spinal column is the sacrum and coccyx. Here nine vertebrae fuse together into two separate bone structures. This area contains six spinal nerves.

If a spinal cord injury occurs in the cervical region, the diagnosis is quadriplegia or weakness of all four extremities. If the injury occurs in other regions, the diagnosis is paraplegia or weakness of the two lower extremities.

What Happens After SCI

The spinal cord can be injured at any area along its entire length (usually by a broken bone of the vertebrae or dislocation of the vertebrae). In general, the higher the level of injury the greater the loss of function. The parts and functions of the body which are located above the point of injury will continue to function unimpaired. The parts and functions which are below the point of injury, however, cannot function in their normal way. Messages from above and below the level of injury are blocked by the damage to the spinal cord and can no longer reach their destination for an appropriate response.

Classification of Injury

Damage to the spinal cord can result in either a complete or incomplete injury. A complete injury results in total loss of motor and sensory function below the level of injury. This implies damage across the entire level of the spinal cord, affecting both the motor and sensory pathways. An incomplete injury results in partial loss of motor and sensory function below the level of injury.

A person has the description of quadriplegia/quadriparesis if damage has occurred in the cervical spinal cord area, resulting in total (plegia), or partial (paresis), loss of motor function in the upper extremities. Paraplegia/paraparesis occurs from damage to the thoracic, lumbar or sacral areas of the spinal cord resulting in lower extremity total or partial loss of motor function.

Level of Injury

A complete Cervical 6, C-6, quadriplegia has intact motor and sensory function at the C-6 spinal segment and above, with all segments below C-6 lost and without motor/sensory functioning. An incomplete C-6 injury has intact motor and sensory function at the C-6 spinal segment and above with partial preservation of motor/sensory function below the C-6 level.

The most common levels of injury are C5-6, T6-7 and T12-L1. Approximately 50% of SCI persons are quadriplegia/quadriparetic and 50% are paraplegia/paraparetic. (See Figs. 4 and 5 for motor and sensory distribution of spinal nerve.)

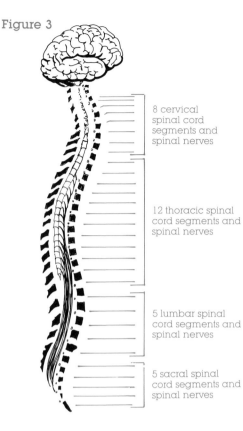

Figure 3

8 cervical spinal cord segments and spinal nerves

12 thoracic spinal cord segments and spinal nerves

5 lumbar spinal cord segments and spinal nerves

5 sacral spinal cord segments and spinal nerves

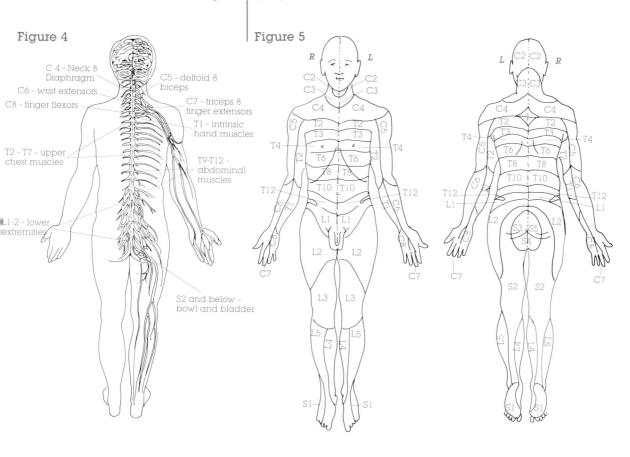

Figure 4

C 4 - Neck 8 Diaphragm
C6 - wrist extensors
C8 - finger flexors
C5 - deltoid 8 biceps
C7 - triceps 8 finger extensors
T1 - intrinsic hand muscles
T2 - T7 - upper chest muscles
T9-T12 - abdominal muscles
L1-2 - lower extremities
S2 and below - bowl and bladder

Figure 5

Functional Levels of Independence in Skiing

L4-5 S-1 Injury: Loss of sensation at the appropriate level, paralysis/paresis of hip extensors, knee flexors and ankle plantar/dorsiflexors. These people are usually ambulators, requiring ankle-foot bracing and forearm crutches or canes. As skiers, these people stand up with support provided by the rigid ski boots and outrigger type ski poles.

L2-3 Injury: Level of sensation moves higher up the body, paralysis/paresis as above with additional involvement of hip flexors and quadriceps or knee extensors; hip adductors may be weak. People often require knee-ankle-foot braces to stabilize the knee and ankle and a pair of forearm or axillary crutches for independent ambulation. A skier requires rigid boots, knee brace and outrigger poles. Many people with this level of injury are sit skiers or mono-skiers.

T7-T12 Injury: Higher level of sensory loss, paralysis/paresis now includes the muscles of the lower back and abdomen. Trunk balance is compromised. Occasionally the person may ambulate with knee-ankle-foot braces and a walker. More commonly the person prefers a wheelchair for independent mobility. The skier is usually a sit skier or mono-skier who functions very well with fair to good trunk balance and good upper extremity strength allowing the use of hand held ``pick'' type ski poles for turning and control.

T1-T6 Injury: This level of injury now involves the upper chest muscles which further compromises trunk balance. Locomotion is essentially limited to a wheelchair. The decreased trunk balance slightly limits independent wheelchair mobility because of an inability to perform ''wheelies'' which permits movement over curbs and other raised obstacles. These people are usually sit skiers and require a velcro type ''torso'' safety strap to maintain an upright sitting position. Without the torso strap people have a tendency to fall forward or sideways and are unable to right themselves easily. This poor trunk balance decreases the skier's ability to make quick, smooth sit skier turns which require the person to alternatively lean from side to side rapidly and plant the ''pick type'' ski pole.

C8-T1 Injury: These people are quadriplegia/quadriparetic depending on the completeness of injury. Hand function is impaired with a decreased ability to flex the fingers and squeeze the hand into a fist. The weak hands make it difficult to adequately grip the ''pick type'' ski poles. Sit skiers with this injury often require a ''kayak-type'' ski pole that is attached to the hand/wrist area by a strap.

C6-C7 Injury: At this level of injury the person has all the above deficits plus weakness of the finger extensors, wrist flexors/extensors, elbow extensors (tricep muscle), and partial weakness of the elbow flexors (bicep muscle). This upper extremity weakness causes a decreased ability to functionally propel a manual wheelchair or use any type of ski pole in an effective turning manner. More responsibility is placed on the sit ski tetherer to help turn the sit ski.

C5-C6 Injury: At this level of injury the person has weakness of the shoulder muscles (deltoids), once again further decreasing the ability to use the upper extremity in a functional way. A powered wheelchair is required for independent locomotion. As a sit skier, the person is unable to use his/her arms for turning maneuvers. He/she is strapped into the sit ski with the arms positioned so they won't get injured and the sit ski tetherer performs all the turning maneuvers. The sit skier essentially goes along for an enjoyable, scenic ride.

C4-C5 Injury and Above: People with this level of injury have no real function except for some head and neck motion. As above under the C6-C7 injury description, the sit skier is unable to perform functional arm ski maneuvers and goes along for a ride.

SCI Skier Special Considerations

Thermoregulation — Impairment in internal temperature control may be seen in persons with spinal cord lesions above T8 and particularly at the cervical level. Adjustment to cooler ambient temperature is low, inconsistent and aided by the amount of cover over the person. This usually does not present a problem for the sit skier or mono-skier who is dressed appropriately. On very cold days the time out on the ski hill should be limited to approximately 2-3 hours with constant checks of the distal extremities. It must be remembered that as a sit skier, the person is sitting close to the snow and usually performing less work, which causes them to feel cold more quickly.

Spasticity — This is manifested by involuntary movements of muscles below the level of the SCI. These movements are due to exaggerated stretch reflex activity that occurs in the healthy portion of the spinal cord below the level of injury. The reflexes are exaggerated because the normal controlling messages from the brain are interrupted by the SCI. For example, if the legs are positioned in a way that stretches muscles, reflex muscle contractions can occur and appear as ''flapping-like'' movements. This reflex activity can be quite uncomfortable for the SCI person. To stop it, simply reposition the leg to reduce the stretch on the affected muscles.

Skin — Sores can easily develop in areas of insensitive skin caused by prolonged pressure over bony prominence areas; (e.g.) ankles, knees, hips, sacrum and ischium (butt bone). All SCI persons have been taught the absolute necessity of avoiding prolonged pressure on the skin by performing weight shirts every few minutes. During sit skiing or mono-skiing activity, the following rules should be observed:

1. Beware of improper positioning in the sled. Have the SCI person sit up straight on the foam cushion in the sled to avoid shearing forces on the sacrum. A shearing force causes greater skin breakdown than a vertical force.

2. Check for areas of increased pressure/pinching. Provide adequate padding; below the heels, between the ankles and knees and under the buttocks.

3. Check that the sit ski or mono-ski safety belts are straight and not twisted, which leads to increased pressure.

4. The quadriplegic person may need assistance in weight repositioning approximately every 30 minutes.

Linda Spies, spinocerebellar degeneration

Bladder Functioning — A SCI can cause a number of control problems in bladder functioning. Each person has an individual program that involves regular emptying of the bladder. Some people have an indwelling catheter (tube) inserted into their bladder. Attached to the other end of the tube is a plastic bag that attaches to a leg and collects urine. This "leg bag" requires emptying when full to prevent urine back-up and bladder distention. The SCI person has been well trained regarding bladder care. The sit skier or mono-skier needs to properly position his/her "leg bag" to prevent pressure on the bag or kinks in the tubing which can cause urine back-up. If a catheter loosens and leaks while skiing, it's important to stop skiing and perform all needed care.

Autonomic Dysreflexia — (Considered an emergency situation.) This condition occurs in persons with a spinal injury usually above the T6 level. It is a hypertensive (high blood pressure) crisis where the SCI person experiences severe sweating, goose bumps, flushed feeling, chilling without fever, severe pounding headache, high blood pressure and increased spasticity. The causes are mainly the problems mentioned above and include: bladder distention from a kinked indwelling catheter or full "leg bag," catheter irritation, skin pressure sores or spasticity from a stretched muscle. If autonomic dysreflexia occurs while sit skiing or mono-skiing, the instructor/tetherer should do the following:

1. Sit the person upright in the sit ski or mono-ski to relieve shearing pressure on the skin.

2. Aid the person in checking the urinary catheter/leg bag for kinks or plugs, if requested or if the person is physically unable to do this.

3. Check for spasticity and if noted, decrease the stretch on spastic muscles.

4. If symptoms continue, get the sit skier down the hill and to the first aid office immediately.

This is an emergency situation and if not managed correctly, could lead to stroke, coma and death. Fortunately, most SCI persons with optimal skin/bowel/bladder care will never develop this problem. Those who have experienced it know the symptoms and can tell you when it's occurring.

Summary

The majority of all SCI persons are young adults who were physically active prior to their injury and since their injury continue to desire athletic challenges. Skiing is one of the most adaptable sports for the handicapped person and can offer enjoyment, challenge and a sense of accomplishment. As with most other sporting activities, skiing has certain inherent risks that are partly responsible for the enjoyment experienced. These risks though must be minimized, especially in the handicapped population. These people have already experienced a traumatic injury with some loss of physical functioning and the last thing they need is another injury resulting in further hospitalization and loss of function. Providing the safest experience possible requires the following: understanding what SCI is, knowing the different levels of injury and the resulting functional capabilities, and knowing the special problems that can be experienced by an SCI person on the ski hill. If all these considerations have been dealt with before the sit skier gets up on the ski hill, unnecessary risk will be minimized allowing for a safe, quality ski day.

Tom Balazy, M.D.
Craig Hospital
Denver, Colorado

Rick Ruscio, member of U.S. Disabled Ski Team.
PHOTO: JEANNE SMITH

Terms of Movement

Flexion — bending
Extension — straightening
Abduction — movement away from the midline
Adduction — movement toward the midline
Pronation — rotate hand or forearm so as to bring palm facing downward
Supination — clockwise rotation of hand or forearm, palm facing upward
Internal rotation — rotation toward the midline
External rotation — rotation away from the midline
Inversion — turning inward, toward the midline
As a treatment technique, head lower than feet
Eversion — turning outward, away from the midline
Rotation — as a treatment technique, twisting trunk off of hips
Motor patterns — the ways in which the body and limbs work together to make movement possible
Sensory-Motor experience — the feelings of one's own movement

Areas and Bones of the Body

Axilla — under the arm
Scapular region — area around the shoulder blades
Pectoral region — front of the chest
Shoulder Girdle (bones of) Scapula — shoulder blades
                    Clavicle — collar bone
Sternum — breast bone
Humerus — upper arm bone
Forearm — extends from elbow to wrist
Radium — one of the two bones of the forearm (thumbside)
Ulna — one of the two bones of little finger side
Carpal bones — eight bones of the wrist
Metacarpal bones — five bones in the hand, corresponding with the five fingers
Phalanges — bones of the fingers or toes
Pollex — thumb
Trunk — body
Gluteal region — hip and buttock
Hip bone — Ilium — large upper part, felt in lower margin of waist
        Ischium — lower part of which body rests in sitting position
        Pubis — anterior part, bone felt at lower part of front of abdomen
Pelvic Girdle — two hip bones together
Iliac Crest — bony ridge below waist
Femur — thigh bone
Acetabulum — cavity in hip bone that receives head of femur
Patella — knee cap
Inguinal Region — groin
Tibia — shin bone
Fibula — calf bone
Malleolus — ankle bone (protuberances on both sides of ankle joint)
Tarsal Bones — seven bones of the ankle
Metatarsal Bones — five bones in the foot
Hallux — big toe
Spinal Column — consists of 33 vertebrae: 7 Cervical vertebrae
                        12 Thoracic vertebrae
                        5 Lumbar vertebrae
                        5 Sacral vertebrae
                        4 Coccygeal vertebrae

Handicapped skiers take a variety of medications for a variety of conditions and reasons. Some medications have side effects that ski instructors should know about. A partial list follows.

Analgesics (other than aspirin and Tylenol)

Narcotics   All have potential for addiction.

Codeine   Given to relieve pain

Demerol   Given to relieve pain
Side Effects: Constipation, depression of cough reflex, addiction

Antibacterial Medications

Furdantin
Macrodantin   Given for urinary tract infection
Side Effects: Nausea, vomiting, diarrhea, dizziness, malaise.

Septra   Given for urinary tract infections. It is a sulfa drug, not for persons allergic to sulfa.
Side Effects: Nausea, vomiting, headache, dizziness, allergic reaction.

Antibiotics

Ampicillin
Penicillin
Oxacillin   Given to treat infection
Side Effects: Diarrhea, nausea, vomiting, skin rashes

Keflex
Keflin
Ancef   Given to treat infections
Side Effects: Headache, malaise, dizziness, nausea, vomiting, abdominal pain, allergies in the form of a rash have sometimes been observed.

Tetracycline   Given to treat infections
Side Effects: Nausea, vomiting, diarrhea, skin rashes.

Gentamycin
Tobramycin   Given to treat serious infections, very powerful, given by injection or in the veins.

Anticholinergics

Daricon   For relief of bladder spasms
Side Effects: Urinary retention, blurred vision, loss of taste, headache, drowsiness, constipation, nausea.

Ditropan   An antispasmodic used for bladder spasms.
Side Effects: Blurred vision, drowsiness, nausea, dry mouth

Anticoagulants

Coumadin   Prevents clotting of the blood — given for leg clots, lung clots
Side Effects: Minor or major hemorrhage from any organ or tissue, dermatitis, fever, nausea, diarrhea

Anticonvulsive Medications

Dilantin   Given to prevent seizures. Commonly used after serious head injury
Side Effects: Slurred speech, mental confusion, dizziness, insomnia, headache, nausea, vomiting, gum enlargement, increased body hair, decreased coordination.

Medications

Phenobarbitol	Given to prevent seizures *Side Effects:* Sleepiness
Depakane	Used to prevent seizures *Side Effects:* Nausea, vomiting, sleepiness
Clonopin	Rarely used to prevent seizures *Side Effects:* Drowsiness, headache

Antiemetic Medications

Compazine	Given to control nausea and vomiting *Side Effects:* Drowsiness, abnormal movements
Phenergan	Given for prevention and control of nausea and vomiting *Side Effects:* Drowsiness, dizziness, dryness of the mouth, blurring of the vision
Vistaril	Given to control nausea and vomiting *Side Effects:* Drowsiness, dryness of the mouth

Anti-inflammatory Medications

Decadron	Potent anti-inflammatory effects in disorders of many organ systems *Side Effects:* Fluid retention, potassium loss, muscle weakness, ulcers, abdominal distention, menstrual irregularities, suppression of growth in children.

Antispasmodic Medications

Used for relief of muscle spasms

Dantrium	*Side Effects:* Drowsiness, dizziness, fatigue, diarrhea, liver injury rarely
Lioresal	*Side Effects:* Drowsiness, dizziness, weakness, fatigue
Valium	*Side Effects:* Drowsiness, fatigue

Hypertensive Medications

Aldactazide	A diuretic medication *Side Effects:* Dryness of the mouth, weakness, lethargy, drowsiness, muscle cramps, hypotension, gastrointestinal symptoms
Apresoline	Given for reduction of high blood pressure *Side Effects:* Continued malaise, chest pain, headache, nausea, vomiting, diarrhea, changes in the blood pressure

Tranquilizers

Minor Tranquilizers Valium Librium Tranxene	For reduction of nervous tension and agitation *Side Effects:* Drowsiness, decreased coordination, dangerous to mix with alcohol
Major Tranquilizers Thorazine Haldol and Others	For severe agitation, powerful drugs used only for specific situations. Many side effects should be discussed with the doctor.

GFL Mono-ski Innovative Recreation, Inc.
P.O. Box 159
Sisters, OR 97759
(503) 549-7022

Mono-ski Bobs Mobility Systems
861 Robinwood Court
Traverse City, MI 49684
(616) 941-4626

**Self-loading
Mono-ski** Woody Witte, Kenny LaCome
Enabling Technologies
2411 N. Federal Blvd.
Denver, CO 80211
(303) 455-3578
(also designing and producing related mono-ski
equipment: seat, outriggers, etc.)

Outriggers Paul's Sports Inc.
124 Columbia Court
Chaska, MN 55318
(612) 448-6987

Sit skis Mountain Man Industries
720 Front Street
Bozeman, MT 59715
(406) 587-0310

Ski bras SKI EZE
4401 Devonshire
Lansing, MI 48910
(517) 882-4608

Slant board William Jackson
7750 Durham Way
Boulder, CO 80301

Smith sled Mountainsmith Products, Inc.
15866 W. 7th Ave.
Golden, CO 80401
(303) 279-5930

Wheelchairs InterMed
9691 S. E. 82nd Ave.
Portland, OR 97266
1-800-367-0674

CLOTHING Rolling Thunder
609 Ala Moana Blvd.
Honolulu, HI 96813
1-800-367-3533 (for catalog, orders)
(A garment manufacturing company that produces fine
fashions for wheelchair-bound people; new lines and
accessories under design)

Martha Hill, National Champion

The 52 Association for the Handicapped, Inc.
441 Lexington Avenue
New York, NY 10017
(212) 986-5281

American Athletic Association for the Deaf (AAAD)
3916 Lantern Drive
Silver Spring, MD 20902

Amputee Sports Association
P.O. Box 60129
Savannah, GA 34120-0129
(912) 927-5408

Blind Outdoor Leisure Development (BOLD)
533 E. Main Street
Aspen, CO 81611

Braille Sports Foundation
7525 North Street
Minneapolis, MN 55426
(612) 935-0423

Breckenridge Outdoor Education Center (BOEC)
P.O. Box 697
Breckenridge, CO 80424
(303) 453-6422

Handicapped Sports Program
Children's Hospital
1056 E. 19th
Denver, CO 80218
(303) 861-6590

Healthsports, Inc.
2455 W. Lake Street
Minneapolis, MN 55408

Horizons for the Handicapped
P.O. Box 2143
Steamboat Springs, CO 80477

International Committee of Sports for the Deaf (CISS)
Gallaudet College
Washington, DC 20002

International Sports Organization for the Disabled (ISOD)
Secretariat CMSH82
CH-1861
Les Mosses, Switzerland

National Association of Sports for Cerebral Palsied (NASCP)
66 E. 34th Street
New York, NY 10016

National Handicapped Sports and Recreation Association
(NHSRA)*
4405 East-West Highway, Suite 603
Bethesda, MD 20814
(301) 652-7505
Mailing Address: 1145 19th St., NW, Suite 717
Washington, DC 20036

National Handicapped Sports and Recreation Association
(Denver Office)*
Capitol Hill Station
P.O. Box 18664
Denver, CO 80218
(303) 232-4575

National Organization on Disabilities
2100 Pennsylvania Ave. NW
Washington, DC 20037
(202) 293-5960

National Wheelchair Athletic Association (NWAA)
660 Capitol Bldg.
301 7th Avenue N.
Nashville, TN 37129

Special Olympics
1701 K. Street NW, Suite 303
Washington, DC 20006

United Cerebral Palsy Association
Sports Coordinator
66 E. 34th St.
New York, NY 10016
(212) 481-6300

United States Association of Blind Athletes (USABA)
55 W. California Avenue
Beach Haven, NJ 08008

United States Cerebral Palsy Athletic Association
34518 Warren Rd., Ste. 264
Westland, MI 48185
(313) 424-8961

United States Deaf Skiers Association (USDSA)
5159 Davis Avenue
Hackensack, NJ 07601

United States Olympic Committee,
Handicapped Sports Committee
750 E. Boulder St.
Colorado Springs, CO 80909-5760
(303) 632-5551

Wheelchair Athletic Association
8597 95th Terrace North
Seminole, FL 33543
(813) 399-1928

*NHSRA currently has 54 affiliated chapters nationwide.
Contact the Washington, D.C. or Denver office for the name
and address of the chapter nearest you.

"My son has had opportunities through the Special Olympics that years ago were available only to gifted athletes. His personal and in-school accomplishments have far exceeded our wildest expectations as a result."

PUBLICATIONS | *This is a very partial list from among many specialty handi-cap publications.*

Ability, Majestic Press, Inc., P.O. Box 5311, Mission Hills, CA 91345. (818) 366-1552. Subscription: $7.00 per year, four issues.

Accent on Living, Raymond C. Cheever, Publisher, P.O. Box 700, Bloomington, IL 61702. (309) 378-2961. Subscription: $6.00 per year, four issues.

A Basic Course in Sign Language, by Tom Humphries, Carol Padden and Terence J. O'Rourke, T.J. Publishers, Inc., 817 Silver Spring Ave., Silver Spring, MD 20910. 1980.

Careers & The Handicapped Magazine, Equal Opportunity Publications, Inc., 44 Broadway, Greenlawn, NY 11740. (516) 261-8899. Subscription: $10.00 per year, two issues.

Challenged American, The National Newspaper for the Disabled, Loy & Loy Communications, P.O. Box 4310, Sunland, CA 91041. Subscription: $6.00 per year, $11.00 for two years, published every other month.

Mainstream, Exploding Myths, Inc., 2973 Beech St., San Diego, CA 92102. (619) 234-3138. Subscription: $14.97 per year, ten issues.

Palaestra, published in cooperation with the United States Olympic Committee's Committee on Sports for the Disabled. Challenge Publications Ltd., P.O. Box 508, Macomb, IL 61455. (309) 833-1902. Subscription: $18.00 per year, four issues.

Dan Pufpaff, International Champion

A Positive Approach, CTEC 1600 Malone St., Municipal Airport, Millville, NJ 80332. (609) 327-4040. Subscription: $10.00 per year, six issues.

Regional Mobility, Regional Mobility Ltd., 401 Linden Center Drive, Ft. Collins, CO 80524. (303) 484-3800. Subscription: $8.00 per year, 11 issues.

Skiing by the Physically Handicapped by Martin H. Krag, M.D. and Duane G. Messner, M.D. Clinics in Sports Medicine, Vol. 1, No. 2, July, 1982. Department of Orthopaedics and Rehabilitation, University of Vermont College of Medicine, Given Building, Burlington, VT 05045

Spinal Network (news journal/resource directory for spinal cord injured). Spinal Network, P.O. Box 4162, Boulder, CO 80306. 1-800-338-5412. Retail: $24.95 plus $3.00 handling.

Sports for the Leg Amputee, by Bernice Kegel, R.P.T. Medic Publishing Co., P.O. Box 89, Redmond, WA 98073. (206) 881-2883. Individual copies: $3.50 each plus $1.25 total postage and handling for up to four copies. Bulk rate (for five or more copies) available.

Sports 'n Spokes, the Magazine for Wheelchair Sports and Recreation. 5201 North 19th Ave., Suite 111, Phoenix, AZ 85015. Subscription: $8.00 per year, 12 issues.

Strategies for Teaching ATS, by Max Lundberg, P.S.I.A., 5541 Central Ave., Boulder, CO 80301. (303) 447-0842. $7.50 per copy for members, $9.75 retail plus $2.00 shipping and handling on all orders. Colorado residents add 3% sales tax.

Amy Cavanaugh, Winter Park instructor, with student   PHOTO: MIKE LEITH

VIDEOS AND FILMS

Training videos for four track, three track, cerebral palsy and sit ski are available for purchase from the Winter Park Handicap Program, P.O. Box 36, Winter Park, CO 80482.

''Two, Three, Fasten Your Ski,'' about amputee skiing; ''The Mountain Does It For Me,'' about neurologically impaired skiing; and ''No Simple Road,'' about children with various physical disabilities, are available for rent or purchase in 16 mm or video format from: Crystal Productions, Inc., P.O. Box 12317, Aspen, CO 81612. (303) 925-8160.

Video on the self-loading mono-ski usage and equipment is available for rent or purchase from: Enabling Technologies, 2411 N. Federal Blvd., Denver, CO 80211.

''Reach for Fitness,'' by Richard Simmons, exercise for the physically challenged, Karl-Lorimar Home Video, 17942 Cowan, Irvine, CA 92714. Suggested retail: $14.95

Diana Goldman, 1987
PHOTO: STEVE STONE

HAL'S PALS

HAL'S PALS began in 1983 as "Bestfriends," a group of dolls with disabilities originated by Audrey Boxwell and Susan Anderson of Fraser, Colorado. Since that time, HAL'S PALS have become recognized and endorsed by experts who work with diverse disabilities, and have appeared in national and international print and broadcast media.

Hal O'Leary was the inspiration for the HAL doll, the signature piece of HAL'S PALS. The disabled dolls have an appealing appearance and cheerful attitude and demonstrate a variety of "can do" challenges. Because the PALS are dolls, children are not threatened when PALS are used to demonstrate information about specific disabilities. The identification of a disabled child with these role models reinforces self-esteem and raises expectations. The conversations about disabilities that the dolls encourage help to remove "disabling barriers" and teach disability awareness to the disabled and non-disabled alike.

HAL'S PALS can be found in homes, hospitals, rehabilitation centers and kindergarten-to-college classrooms. The PALS are used for fundraisers by a variety of national disability organizations and downhill skiing groups.

The product line is expanding to include new additions for classroom use and specially adapted toys. To determine availability in your area, call 303-726-8388, or write to: HAL'S PALS, P.O. Box 3490, Winter Park, CO 80482.

SOURCE: SUSAN ANDERSON

adaptive equipment, 98-103
American Teaching System (ATS), 6, 18-29, 42
amputations, 42-43
arthritis, 122
autism, 125-126

brain, anatomy of, 129
brain injury, 131
bucket, 98
bungi cord, 98

cancer, 123
cant, 99
chair lifts, 36, 49, 59, 68, 83, 91
cerebral palsy, 56-61, 123
cinch, 103
competition, 119

developmentally disabled, 78-81
diabetes, 127
disabled senior citizens, 96-97
disabled skiing history, 15-17
Down's syndrome, 125

epilepsy, 126-127
equipment suppliers, 144

flipskis, 31-32, 45
forms (program), 111-118
four track, 44-55
Friedreich's Ataxia, 127
fund raising, 104-107

Hal's Pals, 149
head injury, 128
hearing impaired, 72-77

learning disability, 131
left hemiplegia, 130-131

medications, 142-143
mental retardation, 124
monoboard, 55, 100
mono-ski, 88-95, 100
multiple sclerosis, 132
muscular dystrophy, 132-133

nervous system, 135-136

organizations, 145-146
outriggers, 30, 44, 101

racing, 13, 119
right hemiplegia, 129-130

shunts, 131
sit ski, 82-87, 101
ski bra, 44, 78, 102
ski buddies, 13
slant board, 102
snow skirt, 101
spina bifida, 133-134
spinal cord injury, 134
Symes amputation, 42

three track, 30-41
toe bar, 103

visually impaired, 62-71
volunteers, 11, 108-110

wedge christie, 21, 24
wedge turns, 18-21, 60, 69
Winter Park Handicap Program, 10-11, 119

Outdoor Books by Cordillera Press

THE OUTDOOR ATHLETE: Total Training for Outdoor Performance
— Steve Ilg
280 pp.   Photos   (6 x 9) $12.95   Softcover   ISBN 0-917895-17-7

TAKE 'EM ALONG: Sharing the Wilderness with Your Children
— Barbara J. Euser
128 pp.   Photos   (5½ x 8½) $11.95   Softcover   ISBN 0-917895-12-6

COLORADO'S HIGH THIRTEENERS: A Climbing and Hiking Guide
— Mike Garratt and Bob Martin
260 pp.   Photos   (5½ x 8½) $11.95   Softcover   ISBN 0-917895-03-7

THE SAN JUAN MOUNTAINS: A Climbing and Hiking Guide
— Robert F. Rosebrough
274 pp.   Photos / Maps   (5½ x 8½) $12.95   Softcover   ISBN 0-917895-07-X

ARIZONA'S MOUNTAINS: A Hiking and Climbing Guide
— Bob and Dotty Martin
180 pp.   Photos   (5½ x 8½) $9.95   Softcover   ISBN 0-917895-18-5

Cordillera Press, Inc.
Post Office Box 3699
Evergreen, Colorado 80439

(303) 670-3010